THE GOSPEL SERIES IN SPIRITUAL SCIENCE

THE GOSPEL SERIES

in

SPIRITUAL SCIENCE

Uncovering The Mystical Connection That
Reveals Your True Relation With God
As The Christ, Your Own Eternal Self

EMMA CURTIS HOPKINS

WiseWoman Press

THE GOSPEL SERIES IN SPIRITUAL SCIENCE:
Uncovering The Mystical Connection That Reveals Your True
Relation With God As The Christ, Your Own Eternal Self.

by
Emma Curtis Hopkins, 1849-1924

Published in 2006

WISEWOMAN PRESS, Beaverton, Oregon

www.wisewomanpress.com

Managing editor: Michael Terranova
Designer & editor: Ruth L. Miller

ISBN: 0-945385-08-0

Metaphysics.
Religion/Spirituality.
Health.

The text in this book was originally published by the Sanctuary of Truth, founded by Dr. Carmelita Trowbridge in Alhambra, California, a leading exponent of the teaching of Emma Curtis Hopkins through the mid-twentieth century. It was her sincere desire that this teaching be a tool for the Spiritual Awakening of all mankind. It is through the efforts of Revs. Shirley Lawrence of the Sanctuary of Truth and Michael Terranova of the Vancouver (WA) Emma Curtis Hopkins Study Center that this current volume has been made possible.

Editor's Note

by Ruth L. Miller, Ph.D.

This is the second in a series of heretofore hard-to-find books by Emma Curtis Hopkins being made available to the general public by WiseWoman Press—and it is a gem. In fact, it may be the most powerful expression of her teaching available today.

In spite of its title, this book is not an analysis of the New Testament stories of Jesus' life and teachings. As usual, Beloved Emma has made the English language serve her purposes to completely reframe the reader's understanding of our nature, the nature of God, and the nature of the Christ. She defines the word, "Gospel," in its original meaning of "Good News," rather than in its currently accepted meaning as one of four books of the New Testament. Still, the Good News that she preaches through these pages is thoroughly founded in biblical scripture—as well as in Hindu and Buddhist texts.

For those who have studied Emma's works, or even Emily Cady's interpretations, the explanation of denials and affirmations presented here will be, at first, familiar—until they see that she is modifying and extending the original statements. That's when the excitement begins to build.

Several new tools and understandings are also offered in this book, including:

- A set of "accusings" to let go of;

- A set of "statements of light" to replace them with; and

- A set of "strengths" that result.

Along with these new tools comes a clear distinction between "intellect" and "mind" and the activities—and results—associated with each.

These new tools, and the amazing insights that go along with them must, inevitably, move the reader who applies them far beyond whatever level of understanding (and power!) than had been achieved before—which is truly Good News! *—rlm.*

Contents

Preface iii

Foreword v

Introduction 1

LESSON ONE 13

LESSON TWO 25

LESSON THREE 37

LESSON FOUR 47

LESSON FIVE 61

LESSON SIX 83

LESSON SEVEN 99

LESSON EIGHT 115

LESSON NINE 133

LESSON TEN 153

LESSON ELEVEN 171

LESSON TWELVE 189

Guidelines for Daily Practice 205

Preface

By Reverend Shirley Lawrence

For those readers who are acquainted with the writings of Emma Curtis Hopkins you will find here another of her insightful explanations of the true teaching of the Christ; for new readers, you have before you a tremendous opportunity for spiritual awakening. Her writing is powerful; she uses language in a new way. You may find that you have to release, even forget, previous ways of thinking and living. But as the hypnotic hold of *societal mind* with its prejudices, fears and mistaken ideas, loosens it grip upon you, the energy of *right ideas* that will fill your consciousness will reveal a whole new world to you.

Emma Curtis Hopkins was born in Connecticut in 1853.[1] Her parents were well educated, especially in history. Emma grew up with books; as a girl she even learned Greek and studied ancient writings in their original language. Through her studies, she became familiar not only with the Old and New Testaments of the Holy Bible, but also with the *Bhagavad Gita,* the *Zend Avesta* of Zoroaster, and the world's great philosophers and saints. This background gave her the strong foundation for her spiritual teaching.

---

[1] While this is the traditional birth date, new records indicate 1849-*ed.*.

She acknowledged three Sciences: Material Science, Mental Science and Mystical Science. The new insights brought forth by such great thinkers as Galileo Galilei, Sir Isaac Newton, and Albert Einstein have given us a truer understanding in the physical sciences, freed from the blind forces of authority and superstition. We have had philosophers throughout history and, in modern times, such men as Carl Jung and Sigmund Freud have given us a better understanding of how the mind works.

But the third science spoken of and taught by Mrs. Hopkins, the *Mystical Science,* "announces the miracles of *'Predicateless Being'* setting the ways of matter at naught and nullifying the thoughts of mind." Thus, the Gospel Series in Spiritual Science explains, in poetic language but clear-cut instruction, the Absolute Principles of the metaphysical universe in which we live Look upon your reading of this book as setting forth upon an exciting spiritual adventure. It will take the student to new levels of *Knowing of God as Changeless Good.*

Pasadena, California
July, 2006

Foreword

By Reverend Marcia Sutton

In 1990 my Spiritual Mentor, the Reverend Lloyd Strom, gave me a copy of the book you are now holding. Although it has taken me many years to realize the Divine Truth that it contains, this book remains the most important one in my library with the single exception of the Holy Bible.

The teachings of Emma Curtis Hopkins have been published in a variety of books and pamphlets. However, *The Gospel Series in Spiritual Science* remains her highest revelation of Truth. Emma spoke from the exalted state of wisdom that the saints and sages of all time have pointed to. She lived from the glorious state of being that Saint Paul proclaimed, "Christ in us." And, she taught from the anointing of love that had the "eyes to see and the ears to hear" the calling of the Absolute.

A strong transmission of Truth is upon this book. It guided and sustained me during the many passages through the "dark night" of my own soul. Emma's words laid down a path for the liberation of my soul in the Light of the Living God. She took me on a journey from the more personal and rational nature of Old Testament metaphysics, known in New Thought as Mental Science, to the more transpersonal and mystical nature of the New Covenant or what is referred to as true Spiritual Science. It was a journey from darkness to light and from living under the rule of the Law or karma to realizing the grace that only God's Love can reveal. Emma's "seeing" guided me step-by-step through the illusion of matter and material existence into and through the gossamer veil of Spirit.

The Truth this book contains represents some of the highest teachings known to humanity. Even though it was written over a hundred years ago, I know it will stand as a beacon of light to spiritual seekers for centuries to come. It is to be savored, studied and shared.

Twelve years after receiving this book, I traveled by myself to Tenerife in the Canary Islands off the coast of Morocco. My intention was to spend each one of the twelve days there in contemplation of a single chapter in this book. By the end of my trip, I had re-read aloud the entire book. I felt that I could finally "see" where Emma had been "seeing" from. In that moment, I was so grateful for the many blessings I had received from my deep and abiding "friendship" in Truth with this beloved founder of the New Thought movement.

Finally, I trust your life will be richly blessed by the inspired words contained within this book. Most importantly, may your life be a living example through which you bring to the world the highest of her teachings.

Portland, Oregon
September 2006

Introduction

I find that my mind is fed by the steadfast gaze I direct toward that Being which is beyond my idea. That which is beyond and out of the range of my thoughts is that which rules my thoughts. That then is God—the true God.

Does not a combination of invisible gases rule water? Is not gas then the ruler of water? Does not water rule the land, forming and unforming it as it decrees? So above and out of the sight and cognizance of land is its ruling principle, the hydrogen and oxygen gases.

I, the embodied thoughts of a life, move and walk by reason of my thought of what is good. But my thoughts are set flowing by the operation of a principle more subtle than thought. What is that which is more subtle than thought? Is it not the vague hope of a good coming to me beyond what has ever yet touched my life? Is not the prime mover of my thoughts then some unnamed good? So God is the unnamed Good.

My thoughts rule my world. They are God over my world. But the unnamed Good rules my thoughts. So by analysis I discover that the God who rules me is never named by me. Can I name that God who has been before unnamed? If I do come to where I name that God who, as nameless Being, rules my thoughts, shall not that name resolve my thoughts back into itself and leave me thought devoid?

And then if by my thoughts I am embodied here in your sight and in my own sight, shall I not disintegrate into formless space by yielding up my thoughts? By the word of the angel, the earth shall dissolve. For the word of the angel is the resolve of thought back into its unnamed expectation of Supreme good, as waters resolved into gases are not visible.

I have been told that at the sound of a tone which they have never heard before, the stones will disappear like shadows. The forces which have held the stones together would be resolved back into the finer essence which the stone expressed. So the rock-bound destiny I fulfill as I stand here the embodiment of my own thoughts, shall melt if my thoughts are resolved back into the name of the Good that no man has named, but which rules all thoughts and all actions.

"Eye hath not seen nor ear heard, neither hath it entered into the heart of man to conceive the things which God hath laid up for them that love him."

I make haste to resolve my thoughts back into the naming of that never-spoken God which has ruled My thoughts, yet itself is not my thought. I willingly keep my thoughts still that the unnamed Good may be named.

As ideas make up my body which I show unto you, I being ready to resolve into my original Good —that which has ruled my thoughts without ruling them—I now surrender my ideas, that having no ideas I may be exalted into the unnamed Good toward which my soul hath forever yearned.

I find that to be beyond my ideas of good is the secret trend of my being. To the good that my thoughts endeavor to move me, I now find I must come by no thoughts. Does the water resolve into its original essentials by flowing on as controlling waters? Does it not touch the gases by the marvelous heat of the chemist jars?

What is that heat to which I may subject my thoughts and resolve them into that of which thoughts are composed? I gladly resolve my thoughts into the anhydrous state of invisible good. What heat shall I use? You need not tell me it is love. For love is the unnamed Good toward which my being is hurrying. Love is but another name for that Good into which I seek to be resolved. It is the nameless expectation of my soul that it shall love its life entirely. Love is the Good itself. But there is some way by which my thoughts may become the constituents of thoughts, as water becomes gases. To this end you study the Science of Christ. To this end I speak and come and go.

It is my believing privilege to believe that there is a quick solution of ideas in the heat of some principle which is not an idea. This principle which shall act with my thoughts as heat acts with water is my power of understanding. My understanding power is finer than my thoughts. My understanding being then my heating power, if I increase my understanding shall I not increase the heat which can resolve my thoughts into that original which is God to my thoughts?

As the fireman puts in more fuel to increase heat, so I put in more fuel to increase my understanding. I find that the fuel upon which my understanding fire is fed is a fine white substance generated by words of Truth as electric charges are generated by batteries. Words which deal with any subject generate a substance in the airs. Words which deal with such subjects as money, houses, lands, children, temperance reforms, prisons, schools, etc, generate a coarse substance which causes the understanding of mankind to heat up with coarse tastes. Thus mankind likes beef and lamb to eat; cows and dogs to clothe itself with, swine and whales to handle with its hands. These things suggest coarse thoughts again. The thoughts discourse upon them still again. So round and round the coarse products turn themselves.

Words concerning the character of a Being who thinks of none of the things the words of matter suggest generate a finer substance for a finer understanding power to feed on. They make a heat which is seven times hotter than the talk of swine and soldiers. This heat begins to cause my thoughts to refine as heat causes water to refine into steam. I will keep on telling of Christ and God till my words are so true that they generate a substance finer than any that any understanding has ever fed on. Thus I will be the chemist standing here at the laboratory of my mind and resolving my thoughts back into gases. I will have no thoughts with which such a world of beggars and deaf and blind men and women can be made. I will become in the estate of my own consciousness that which I am in fact at the head of my Being—I will be that God which rules thoughts . . . exalted into my Self.

This exaltation is not fed by an understanding of opposites. It is fed on knowing that I AM now come into my own estate. I stand here and speak of my

Self. Of my original element which is the unnamed Good I speak. My body is quickened. It is made of that which is finer than thoughts of material things and finer than thoughts of numbers and logic. It is fed on my understanding of God. It is a new body in my new understanding. This is Transfiguration.

I take by choice thoughts which all the world call the mountain peaks of thought. These are of God, who is finer than understanding of God. I keep them going in the wheeling batteries of my mind. They generate a substance upon which my understanding feeds. This understanding is hot. It melts my old thoughts and dissolves my old body. It then takes new thoughts of God. And beyond itself generates a newer substance so white—fuller and whiter than anything on earth. A finer and clearer understanding breaks forth. It speaks and I see what body God created. I am in the understanding of God. This is rest. This is the rest of God. It is action so swift that it is no action at all. I seem to be doing nothing. I seem to be thinking nothing. But my fine true thoughts heating my understanding till it dissolves thoughts is swiftly putting me into my transfigured body of God. It is by Spiritual Science reasonings that I generate that substance which feeds understanding.

All that has ever been accomplished of greatness and goodness and beauty has been brought to pass by true words generating a substance fine and white which fed understanding till great things came to pass by its word.

The heaven of freedom sought for by the Buddhas of old cometh clearly visible by melting the bands of the chains of thinking of good and evil.

It is not heaven to be famous among men. To be chained to the hope of fame is to be hitched like a dog to the chariot of Mercury, the star of fame. Dante, the poet, generations ago discovered that to be thinking of fame is to generate a substance that feeds understanding with a fuel that is heating fuel as coarse though more subtle than looking for shoes and wagons of matter. He calls the exercise of thoughts striking their wheels against each other to make praise of mankind the destruction of freedom. He tells how the mind which looks for praise of mankind never shines by its own light but reflects the light generated by the appreciation of fellow beings. A man's fellow-beings are thus more in the cause of truth by seeing his powers than he is himself. He clashes his thoughts and words together and the people catch the fine meanings he carries. Their pleasure pleases him. But he has eaten none of his own manna. If you are depending upon praise or appreciation you are not fed by the true manna. Understanding is not fed with its right fuel, so its heat does not melt your thoughts.

On his mind stairs Dante kept ascending by thoughts, and thus explained why the brilliant genius is so often unhappy and restless. He gets his pleasure only in praise. Even with the Mercurial religious saint, says Dante, we cannot tell how much his religion is genuine. His religion is bright like the noon sun. He tells of the doctrines of that religion. His hearers feel how true it is and praise him. But he has not felt his understanding fires burn and so his thoughts of worldly things do not melt.

Do you feel troubled if success of enterprise does not attend you? If so, then surely it is success of enterprises upon which you are trying to feed your understanding fires.

I am not here to be fed on the manna fuel generated by talk of prosperity, by talk of healed bodies, say the Divine fire which can melt my thoughts into gases. I yield all things to the Spirit of Understanding for the sake of being resolved into love. God is love.

By love I do not mean the feeling experienced by those who adore some man or some woman or some child clothed in what seems to be flesh. This is the heaven of the planet Venus, says Dante. It is narrow and surrounded by the high banks of never wishing to leave the earthly ways. The love that is the good toward which my heart is forever yearning is not named in the earth. Nothing is resting in the love which it feels for one in the flesh. It always fears something will happen. The love that my thoughts are losing their life for is the love that has never heard of apprehension. Thus is God exalted in my hope above love.

The God who rules my hope is the presence of the happy kingdom into which I am exalted when I do not think of things that are material any more at all; neither do I think of life, or truth, or love. I look beyond my ideas into the great Fact of Life. This looking into Life, the great fact, away from my idea of life is the dissolution of my ideas. I willingly see my ideas dissolved in my sight by the inner God of my Being looking straight out over the universe of God folding me here. I am at the center of my being called to look out upon God. "Look unto Me."

The whole secret of freedom is in silent looking. As Mary looked beyond all ideas into the God beyond ideas she brought forth Jesus Christ. As I look into the home that is beyond my ideas I bring forth home for the people of earth. As I look into the God who is support beyond my idea of sustaining and supporting I bring forth the plenty I see as I look.

There is a power of my mind called "looking" by which I am able to see what is beyond my thoughts. While I am looking at God as One who knows nothing of supporting me, I find myself saying, "God is my support." After speaking this truth I have new clothes, new home conditions, new strength. Now if I had spoken the words over many times that God is my support before I had dropped the idea of support and looked beyond my idea, I should have had to wait for my words to generate the white Substance for fuel to my understanding. Then my understanding would have looked in silent adoration at the God who is beyond understanding and I should have spoken the words, "God is my support," after a long time of waiting.

I have by this manner of thinking come to see that I need not generate the fuel for my understanding to flame by if I do not choose. I may look straight past all ideas into that which is not idea. And then I shall be thinking the vital principle that makes health but never speaks of health. I am the speaker of health.

Mary returned from her speechless sight of Good beyond her ideas of good and spoke of Messiah. I now return from my speechless sight of Good beyond my ideas of good and I speak that all is the unresisted action of the Living Spirit through all the earth now.

I now return from my speechless sight of Good beyond all ideas of good and proclaim that the Healing Spirit is now acting with unresisted freedom through you all and through all the earth now. This is the loss of my ideas in the unnamed Good. It is the re-finding of my ideas in the nameless Good. I have willingly let go all ideas to be lost in the Good My unthinking mind sees.

I obey the one injunction I have heretofore omitted, *viz.*, "Look unto Me and be ye saved, all the ends of the earth."

As Mary brought forth Jesus by her immaculate sight of Good, I by my immaculate sight of Good say now that the strengthening Spirit is acting with unresisted freedom through all the earth and you now.

This also is Jesus Christ. The movement of the Spirit of that which is beyond thought makes thought.

My sight of there being a good beyond the excitements of the ideas and feelings I now apprehend finally gets immaculately free from the dust of My opinions of material things and unspiritual ideas. This is forgetfulness of matter and thoughts. Pure forgetfulness is immaculate sight of the Good that has never been named. The sight of that Good formulates new environments. They are the perfect conditions which alone can rest my heart. Perfect conditions are Jesus Christ come again. So I bring forth Jesus Christ to this age. My Jesus Christ is a whole world in the same estate of power and life and understanding as Jesus Christ had and does have and forevermore shall have.

I must know a good higher than blessing God for giving me something He does not give you. God does not give and withhold. He is above giving and withholding. He hears no thanks offered from a mind that feels he is capable of giving and not giving at one and the same moment. I believe in God beyond God. The God beyond God is His nature toward whom My heart panteth, toward whom my feet tend.

These words generate a fine light. On that light my understanding feeds. I understand God, there I am dissolved.

The stillness of the unnamed Good stands in my presence. I am as silent as it is silent. Suddenly my voice shall break forth with a new tongue. I will come down from the high stillness into speech as a river flows down from its mountain. As water falls down from its gases. From the everlasting calm of the good beyond thoughts I bring you this word. God cannot be exalted. God is abiding in stillness which is "in hell and on earth."

The sounds on the shores of time disturb not the silence of God. My excitements of pleasure or pain touch not the stillness of the God beyond God, dwelling within my being.

I AM above goodness I AM beyond wisdom; I AM beyond virtue; by reason of the everlasting mountain and valley and sea and land of stillness abiding in me. This is not lifting up or putting down.

It is the mystery of Everlasting Kindness.

Emma Curtis Hopkins

Omnipresent Omnipotent Omniscient

Reasoning from the standpoint that I am of the same substance as my Creator, I find I am obliged to say that there is no other substance except that which my Creator is; for my Creator, which is God, fills heaven and earth.

"Do I not fill Heaven and Earth?" [Jeremiah 23:24]

LESSON ONE

The Knowledge of God
As Changeless Good

1. If you will notice the next thought in your mind after speaking forth definitely the first and indestructible idea that there is good for you, and that this good is your God, Omnipresent Substance, reliable, eternal, you will see it is now natural for you to say that in your idea of good there is no mixture of evil.

2. This feeling that comes up so surely when describing your Good or your God, had led many thinkers to speak out boldly that in reality there is no evil whatsoever.

3. It is good reasoning which insists that in Omnipresent Good there can be no evil. The whole matter of dealing with mind is soon found to be the necessity for speaking and thinking consistently.

4. We are working out a common problem. It is the problem of Life. The well-known answer to the problem is satisfaction. Satisfaction is best defined as health, judgment, prosperity.

5.   When we take the common idea prevailing that there is good for us which we ought to have, we have in our mind the word "good." Hold this word "good" in mind and soon you will feel the necessity for naming your good. This naming of the good is the statement of beginning—Origin. Out of this good, out of the very Word Itself all things are made. "The Word was God—the Good, and without Him was not anything made;" that is, every movement, every speech is made, expecting good to come visible and thus the word "good" governs all, moves all, makes all, causes all.

6.   In every mathematical problem there is a principle involved with which we must deal accurately if we would see the right answer. A problem in life demands exactly that accurate handling. Jesus Christ started out saying, "I and My Father are One." Father means Origin. First Cause. Have you started out by saying, "I and the Good are One"? If from this Good we come forth, then we are It.

7.   Since we are indeed the true Substance, we would naturally expect that to say we were of any other substance than Good, which is God, would make some havoc with our life problem. It would be bringing in another substance to handle besides Spirit and thus we must have an unreliable, transient, changeable substance to think of, just the opposite of Spirit.

8.   It is not surprising that we have change and decay to deal with if we have spoken of a substance not Spirit. Thus it is, that from the standpoint of righteousness, the right thinking have said boldly: "There is no matter." By this they mean that they will be truly righteous in dealing with the one

substance, God, who is Spirit Omnipresent, and will say that in a universe occupied by Spirit only, occupied by God only, there is no room, nor space, nor place, nor where, for any other substance.

9.   "Am I not God?" "Do I not fill heaven and earth?" God is Spirit everywhere and God is Changeless Good everywhere. Then there is no evil anywhere and no matter anywhere. God is everywhere.

10.   These are the first two denials the mind makes when it is not paying attention to anything, to any idea, save what is true. It is as sure to put evil out of our view to declare its unreality, as it is to put a wrong combination on the slate out of sight, when we draw a wet sponge over it. All things are made out of words. The spoken word is the prompt creator of all things. The spoken word may be silently spoken or audibly spoken, but it is what we put into words that we experience. It is only when we put the good into words that we speak what is true. Thus all that is not good is not true. Only the good is true. An untruth has no foundation. It has no principle. It has no substance. Nothing that is made of an untruth has a foundation. It has no principle. It has no substance. Nothing that is made of an untruth is worthwhile. So Jesus Christ said, "The flesh profiteth nothing!" "The words that I speak unto you, they are Spirit and they are Life."

11.   When Jesus Christ told all who heard him or who should hear him, forever to deny themselves, he meant, of course, for them to deny what was not true. He certainly did not mean for them to deny themselves of food and clothing and friends, for he ate and drank and dressed himself like the

rest of them. What he was talking about was words.

12.   In Truth there is no evil. In Truth there is no matter. In My Good there is no mixture of evil. In My Good there is no failure. In My Spirit there is no failing substance.

13.   Reasoning from the standpoint that I am of the same Substance as My Creator, I find I am obliged to say that there is no other substance except that which My Creator is, for My Creator who is God, fills heaven and earth.

14.   Then when I say Spirit is all and matter is nothing, I am not destroying matter nor material things, for there is no matter to destroy. All is Spirit. My denial is simply My true word which I speak. It is the simplest justice I can render My Creator to give Him in His perfect Substance, all place, all power, all wisdom, all truth. It is the realization of Truth by My mind, and I am only speaking forth what I know is true. Then is fulfilled in every one who speaks this Truth, the freedom which Jesus Christ promised to all who should speak their knowledge of Truth. "Ye shall know the Truth, and the Truth shall make you free." What the mind realizes is all the hearing power there is. What the mind realizes is all the seeing and feeling power there is. What the mind realizes of Life is all the living there is. Can you not see that if mind realizes all Life, that all Life is possible to the mind?

15.   Who realizes and knows all things? God. Where is God? Everywhere. With what does God know and realize all things? With mind. What is there for God to be conscious of and realize except Spirit? Nothing. Is it possible that there is anything for God to see that He does not see? No. God

would not be all-knowing or Omniscient if He were incapable of seeing some of His own creation. He created all things. But it is written that "He beholdeth not iniquity" and surely—"Iniquity doth abound." The reason that it is written He "beholdeth not iniquity" is because there is none for Him to behold. The standpoint from which one would say that "iniquity abounds" is from the standpoint of a lie.

16.   There is no satisfaction in having two substances or two principles opposed to each other in our mind. The standpoint of one God and His name "One", or one Substance and His name Spirit, brings freedom and peace forth from the Truth to be visible to us. The third denial that is natural and reasonable, if we have spoken forth our conviction boldly that in our idea of Good there is no mixture of evil and in our idea of Spirit there is no matter, is, "There is no absence of Life, Substance or Intelligence." Since God is Omnipresent Life then Life is never absent. The sights of the flesh profit nothing because they are all made out of lies. Every material sight which fails is the product of speaking of evil and matter. Remember that it is good to speak Truth. It is not good to speak untruth.

17.   It is Truth to say in Spirit, "There is no matter," and as Spirit is everywhere, matter must be nowhere. There is no matter. It is good to say this and no transient imperfect substance will ever come into view if we hold this word. It will lead to our insisting that Life is never absent, and as the saying that death is present and has possession is sure to get hold of some one by the law and nature of words in their manifesting quality, it is also sure

that to say, "Life is not absent," will fill and thrill the most dead looking object that ever came, seeming to be real. If you see death with the eyes and feel it with the hands, that does not signify anything but that you have thought that Life might be absent. You might as well say that God is absent as to say that Life is absent, for Life is God.

18.   The good Life that you praise never mixes itself with death. There is no idea of death mixed with the true idea of Life. There is only one Principle of action and that is Life. There is no absence of Life. To wash the mind of its notion of death is to leave Life in full sight. God is the only Substance. There is no absence of God. There is no absence of Substance. Nobody is ever absent from us. No good thing is absent from us. Good is never absent, Prosperity is never absent. It is the same as saying God is absent to say that prosperity is absent.

19.   It is not Truth to speak of the absence of prosperity. To name our absence of prosperity by such words as poverty, lack, want, is to speak what is so untrue that great havoc is made with our life problem. Then we wonder why we are so poor, so far from prosperity, so far from tangible Good. Nothing but Truth will give us a hold on that good, for Truth and tangible Good are One. There is no absence of the God Substance. There is no absence of the Life Substance. Our idea of prosperity has no mixture of failure or absence. Our idea of good is that it is never absent. Our idea of good intelligence is that it is never absent. Reliable, steadfast, changeless Intelligence is the Omnipresent God. God, the Omnipresent Intelligence of the universe is never absent. To let the idea of the absence of Intelligence get mixed with our idea

of Omnipresent Intelligence, is to have the appearance of foolishness and ignorance sometimes among us.

20.   But the appearance of foolishness and ignorance being only the out-showing of our false notion about absence, there is no reality in it. There is no foundation for foolishness and ignorance. There is no principle of reasoning to base them on. "Judge not according to appearances" at all. Judge reasonably. People will willingly judge reasonably the instant they find that all tangible things depend upon words.

21.   And people will gladly speak forth the truth concerning their idea of Intelligence as not mixed with foolishness and ignorance when they realize how visible their own wonderful Intelligence will be to all the worlds when once the truth is told that there is no absence of Intelligence. It does not destroy foolishness and ignorance to declare that they cannot be real because Intelligence is unmixed. There is nothing to destroy.

22.   Intelligence is the Omnipresence. Where shall we find anything non-intelligent within Intelligence? It cannot be done. It is only speaking honest truth to declare that there is no absence of God. Then as God is Intelligence it is only speaking honest truth to declare that Intelligence is never absent.

23.   Nothing is changed or destroyed by this Truth. Truth is left in its glory all uncovered of imaginations of what is not true. Thus you see how we have come by the third denial demanded of the mind by Truth: viz. There is no absence of Life, Substance or Intelligence. There was another way of putting this denial which was not so easily rea-

soned out or explained though it meant just the same. It was this way: There is no Life, Substance or Intelligence in matter." This made it seem as if it was a very righteous thing to drive Life, Substance and Intelligence from the body.

24.   Now the only body there is, is Spirit. The only body there is, is God. So all the objects and all the people are full of God and there is no absence of God. It is no use to call God by a material name and suppose that makes Him absent. There is no use speaking of a stone as lacking Life, for Life is as quickened in the presence we call stone as in the archangel.

25.   There is no use saying there is no substance in our body because our body is Spirit. Our body is not material substance; it is God-Substance. Our body is every bit of it quickened by Life, by Intelligence, and is filled with God-Substance.

26.   We are the temple of God, filled and shining with God. Here Paul says: "Know ye not that Jesus Christ is in you?" Jesus Christ means Word of Truth. Know ye not that the Word of Truth is in you? Speak this Word of Truth. Then you are Life, Substance, Intelligence, Omnipresence. There is nothing so efficient to work as Truth. Truth is Science.

27.   According to Science (Truth) there is no absence of Life, Substance, Intelligence. According to Science, which is knowledge of Truth, there is no evil. According to what you know of Truth, there can be no reality whatsoever in evil or in material things and no absence of Life, Substance or Intelligence.

28. God is the Life Omnipresent, the Substance
Omnipresent, the Intelligence Omnipresent. There
is a fourth reasonable conclusion within your
mind. Speak it:

There is nothing to hate.

God is Love. God fills all things. As you cannot
hate the Good that is in you, so you cannot hate
God, for the good that is for you is your God. The
good that is for you is the life, substance, intelligence, health, prosperity, everything for you. Everything is good, and quickeningly good for you.
"There is nothing to hate."

29. Is it not your own idea of good that it never
fails you anywhere or under any circumstances?
If it ever gives you a stone when you want bread,
then it fails you. So if your idea of good is carried
out in its perfection, there is no such thing as failure, by the agency of something you call hardness
or failure of good.

30. The hardest seeming man or woman is
filled and thrilled with Soul. This is Truth. According to science, Soul is God Omnipresent. God is
joy. God is bliss. "In Him is fullness of joy." And
thus as God is no more in one place than another
all things are the bliss of God, and there is nothing
to hate.

31. It is your idea of good that it shall never be
absent. It is your idea of good that it shall have
nothing in it to hate. If you speak this denial as it
is written in your mind it will be: "In My idea of
good there is nothing to hate." Then if you speak it
more abstractly and impersonally you will say that
in the good there is nothing hateful—nothing to
hate. But that is only explaining the reasoning by

which you and all the world when speaking honestly, come to the conclusion that there is nothing to hate.

32.   This denial has been expressed in these words: "There is no sensation in matter." This scientific denial has needed a great deal of explaining. The Truth that Spirit is all sensation, has made it seem as if we must drive sensation from somewhere in order to be scientific. It seems by this denial as if our bodies should be denied sensation. But our only body is Spirit. Spirit is alive and quickened with consciousness. Sensation is pure consciousness. Spirit is always conscious. Thus we are filled and thrilled with sensation. We are filled and thrilled with consciousness. There is no more absence of sensation than there is absence of life.

33.   The best denial when toothache seems to thrill you with something to hate is this: "In Spirit there is no toothache. There is nothing to hate. In Spirit all is peace. In Spirit all is delight.

34. Now you and I and all things are Spirit; we are not matter. Spirit is God. All is God. It is useless to try to make out that there is anything except God. God is all.

Omnipresent Omnipotent Omniscient

In the Beginning the "Word was God" or Good:
That is within mind, where the thoughts start.
The Word was and Is and ever more shall be
Good.

"In the beginning was the Word and the Word was with God, and the Word was God." [John 1:1]

LESSON TWO

The Law of Words

1.   Everywhere is this conviction of good which belongs to us. And this good must be present, to be as good as we think it might be. Then do not hesitate to speak of your highest ideal of Good. This is, that it is never absent. If I were to speak the Truth as it comes to me, I should be saying: "

> My Good, that is what I should like and ought to
> have, is not mixed with anything hateful.

Jesus Christ touched us all right at this idea of what we would like and told us to speak of ourselves as already having it.

2.   Good is a word that is healthy and strengthening for the mind to hold.

3.   Now it is easy to see that if anything is already here, the use we get of it, or the comfort we get of it, depends upon whether we see it or do not see it. It is one of the fundamental statements that we state very definitely that in our idea of the good there is no mixture of evil. There is no mixture of failure. There is no absence of Life, Substance or Intelligence. There is nothing to hate. The second

denial as we have put it: "There is no matter," is apt to put money and friends away from us, houses and lands away from us, if we have looked upon them as matter.

4.   Remember all is Spirit.   Houses and lands are Spirit, money and friends are Spirit.   They are not matter.   So some had better say, "Nothing is matter," instead of 'There is no matter.'" The belief of matter and the ways of matter lead to sin, sickness and death in material things and people. All these oppose the Good. Hence some have put this second denial in this way:

There is no opposition to the Good.

There is no opposition to God. Then there is no devil. There is no opposition to Spirit is a beautiful denial for people who have trouble along any line. The Spirit is ready to do everything good for the mind that tells the Truth about it. "Truth is mighty and will prevail." This is the Truth. Speak it: "There is no opposition to Spirit. There is no opposition to Good. There is no opposition to Truth."

5.   Remember that it is a belief in things being made of matter that has covered our planet with things dying and with things to hate. Truth lifts this veil.

6.   Which denial of matter pleases you most? Which sets you free as you speak it? Good is never absent. There is no matter. There is no failure of Good. There is no failure. There is no opposition to Good. There is no opposition to Spirit. There is no opposition to Truth. There is no opposition. There are those who say, "Things are not matter, they are Spirit."

7. It is sure that while we believe in the reality of matter, we get the sight and sounds and experiences of poverty, death, disease, decay and trouble.

8. In an Egyptian cave were found printed these words: "Truth is not cumbered by matter." It means the same as the one used for ages which would have shown forth in freedom from all opposition, if it had been followed by an honest statement that in our idea of Good there is no absence of Life, Substance or Intelligence and there is nothing to hate.

9. The word makes or brings forth all that we say. We choose what we shall speak. We cease from speaking of what is not good. The word is responsible for all things. Do you find any idea of sin, sickness, death mixed with your idea of good? Are they good according to your idea of good? Why do you not say so then?

10. In my idea of good there is no sin, no sickness, no death. In my Good there is no sin, sickness, death. Do you not see how metaphysicians have come by their bold denial called the fifth denial:

> There is no sin, no sickness, no death in my idea of
> the good.

All things and all people have the same idea of good. The idea is omnipresent. The word good is an omnipresent idea. Spoken out and described, it manifests itself in all things. All is Good. The spoken word fulfills it. It all rests upon the speaking or not speaking of the word good.

11. 'In the beginning the Word was God" or Good. That is within the mind, where the thoughts

start. The Word was and is and ever more shall be Good.

12.   There is no possibility of ever being sick if the denials of science have ever been spoken with honest knowledge that they are true. There is no such thing as a sight or experience of death if ever we have spoken the denials of science with our mind single to the truth of them.

13.   They are like a washing of the mind by water. They are the real water baptism. They are the cleansing of the mind by the blood of the Lamb. Blood means Living Word and the Lamb means meek Truth. Nothing shows meekness like the honest giving up of all our old ideas for what we see is really the true idea within the deep place of our heart.

The Blood baptism is the sacrifice of old ideas; it is like a fire, cleansing by burning away our old rubbish.

Do not be surprised if when you begin to speak the denials of science, you actually feel as if all the old landmarks were being washed away. Do not be surprised if you feel as if you were in some mysterious way sacrificing some vital points. Do not be surprised if you feel as if fires were cleansing you.

14.   Remember you do not believe in evil and there is no evil working with you, for you or by you. Resist not the Divine Good as it works through you.   Resist nothing. Non-resistance to evil lets it fall harmless outside your door. Non-resistance to good lets it stream like a great river of kindness and bounty through your premises.

Naaman washed seven times in the River Jordan to symbolize our denials.

We have to make two other denials besides the five already mentioned, the last two are very necessary. You may have had such a severe life or may be having certain ideas that will bring great severity into your lot in life. The denials of science are a great preparation for prosperity. Many persons make this one of their denials:

I am not personality.

Do you know that you are Spirit? Person means mask or deceit. Spirit is no deceiver.

15. For the second personal denial many use this:

There is no burden on my spirit.

What causes the burden on the mind? It is a belief in sin and sickness. It is the conscience within that arises and accuses. So some have said:

There is no accuser within me.

16. Every statement of Being or Origin or Beginning should have the word Jesus Christ at the close of the statement, because that name means, "This has been demonstrated."

17. "In Jesus Christ is all fullness of the Godhead bodily."

18. The denials are the words of Jesus Christ. He demonstrated every one of them. All matter was nothing to Him. All evil was made nothing to Him and by Him. All disease, sin, pain, death, poverty were nothing to Him. He said He had put them all under His feet. He was the Truth and the Word of Truth. He was the living statement of Being or acknowledgement of Good and the living denial of evil and matter. His Name means demonstration of Life. His Name means absolute demonstration of

Good by word and life. His Name means all that we can think of that is power and judgment and success. Everything He did, He did because he chose to do it and not because it mastered or compelled Him. He was master of all the world. You are not to experience anything at all of evil or pain or poverty, if you keep His Name as the living fulfillment of all the denials of science. He said, "Keep My words." Hush your thoughts and hear Him speaking these words through the stillness of your own mind.

19.   Say boldly: "All power is given unto Me." "I have overcome the world." There is no power in evil. "Thou couldst have no power at all except it were given thee from above." There is therefore no power except God.

20.   Matter profiteth nothing. Wherever My Good Word is sent, you will see sin lost, sickness done, forgotten. The grave and death are forgotten. The Good shall wipe away all tears from the eyes.

The word Good is already in your mind and I have already demonstrated it. When sorrow comes to you, refuse the cup. I took it and I assure you that there is no virtue or credit in thinking sorrow belongs to you. "When death comes claiming your loved ones, refuse the cup." "I tasted death once and found it no part of Life." When poverty comes, refuse the cup. I tasted poverty once and found it all delusion.

In the Good there is plenty and to spare. God is Love. Love makes your life easy. When anything comes claiming to belong to you that would hurt you, say boldly in my Name and by my authority: "I refuse the cup. Jesus Christ told me I need not drink it."

21. You will find this Truth will bring angels to fight your cause as they fought for Elisha. Angels are perfect thoughts in action.

22. The regular announcements of what is true, are all the time working with us and for us and by us, but when the daily delusions caused by words we formerly spoke, come round us, we may say:

> I refuse them. Put far from me sorrow and pain. Put far from me all human experiences that Jesus Christ told me I need not bear.

This is the clearing of my mind from its errors as the cloud parted the earth when the planet was dividing the waters from the waters.

23. Moses saw this and said: "Let there be light." The light within is the Truth within. The light without is the Truth without. The Truth is One. The within and without are one. The Truth is within us. Open all the gates of the mind. The second gate of the mind is its denial of all mixtures of evil with its good. Swing boldly open the gates of denial. Regard no appearance against your holiest convictions.

24. It is when appearances formed by error combat our reasoning of what ought to be, that we do not speak boldly if we listen to what claims to be true, but is not true. Only the good is true. Only what is unmixed good, is the outward signal of that boldly spoken truth which is written on the tablets of our own mind waiting to be spoken.

25. No external process will give us a sight of Good. No legislation, no combination of charitable movements, no philanthropic scheme will work the sight of the Kingdom of Heaven into our eyes. The

deep things of the soul—of the heart—must be rea-
soned out or told aloud definitely, if they are to be
seen as the accomplished experiences.

26. We make our world by our words. But only
that world is real and true which is good. Thus
only true words have any reality in them. All true
words are those which tell of what ought to be.
That which our Soul knows of what ought to be, is
that which Is. All that we feel ought not be, is not.

27. This world that appears to our senses and
has power to hurt, is not real. It is the product of
our saying that what ought not be, is. All great
minds refusing to believe in the necessity for evil
have come to one conclusion. This is their conclusion: "There is a Kingdom on the earth though it is
not of it — a kingdom wider than the bounds of the
earth though they were rolled together as finest
gold and spread by the beating of hammers."

28. Why must this Kingdom be so wide? To
take in the innumerable company of those who
have washed their robes white. Robes are the covering of the Soul. We wash these thought robes
clean by Truth. Truth is written within our hearts.

29. Only those who speak Truth can enter into
the sight of the glory of the Kingdom of Heaven or
the true world at hand, where there shall not be a
lying tongue found among all its inhabitants.

30. All that hides us from the sight of our everlasting Home is the neglect to speak forth the denials within our mind. The denials are like the
parting of curtains. The denials lift the veil of delusion from our faces. We waken. The nightmare of
human experience closes. We do not die but we

open our eyes and find that all is as a dream that claimed to be pain, disappointment, misfortune.

31.   In Isaiah we find prophecies of this teaching.   It is said: "After that, one shall come who shall not judge after the sight of the eyes, nor after the hearing of the ears, that an ensign shall be lifted up and unto it all the nations shall come." All nations have this law written within their mind and deep in their hearts. They all love the good and choose that in their good there shall be no mixture of evil.

32.   It is by this bold word we now speak that what is unmixed Good will be seen. It is the White Stone of Revelation. Look at it. It has been demonstrated by Jesus Christ and Jesus Christ waits with loving majesty in every part of the universe for your words of denial to part the curtains of delusion, to rend the veil of error, to refuse to believe in any other Presence or Power or Intelligence save God only.

33.   The veil must be rent by our own words. The delusion must be scattered by our words. Moses speaks as if the earth must do something to swing into the sunshine. "Let there be light" as if the earth were holding down her own veil. The earth is mind. Hear the prophecy which now we fulfill! "He will destroy the face of the covering cast over all people, and the veil that is spread over all nations. He will swallow up death in victory. And the rebuke of his people shall be taken away from off all the earth."

34.   It has been our rebuke that we have not let our highest convictions rise to proclaim themselves

as boldly as our suppositions and suspicions have been spoken.

35.   The Lord taketh away this rebuke. The Lord is the Law of the Good spoken. When the Good is spoken, it is the law that it is seen. God is Good. There is only God. God is Good. There is nothing unlike God. God is Spirit. There is nothing unlike Spirit.   God is Good. God is Life, Truth, Love. There is no absence of Life, Truth, Love, Substance, Intelligence. God is Joy. There is only God. I am not personality. God is Love manifest in Jesus Christ. There is no burden on My Spirit. "My yoke is easy and My burden light." With those words "The former heaven and the former earth shall be forgotten; neither shall they come into mind anymore."

36.   There is no use holding back your noblest convictions, now that you know the Law of words. Now words are seen in things. "Without the Word was nothing made that was made."

Omnipresent Omnipotent Omniscient

Truth is the Light that shines when the True God is named.

"Thou art the God even thou done of all the kingdoms of the earth."   [Isaiah 37:16]

LESSON THREE

Gospel Lesson on Hezekiah
[Isaiah, Chapter 37]

1.   Truth is omnipresent and will prevail. Any mind that stops all its thinking, except true thinking, will find that the truth he thinks will do remarkable works. As to the destruction of error there is no telling how the mighty miracle will be wrought. But it is certain that no error can stand in the presence of the statement of the mighty Truth.

2.   In the 37th Chapter of Isaiah we are told how Hezekiah, King of Judah, received a letter from Sennacherib, King of Assyria, stating that if Hezekiah would yield Jerusalem and all his Kingdom to the Kingdom of Assyria, there would be no more want and no more trouble to the Jews. Hezekiah noticed that Sennacherib had reminded him of the many nations that had been obliged to yield by force of arms to Assyria, when they had presumed to stand out against his demands for surrender. Sennacherib said that it was no use for Hezekiah to hope for any assistance from his God out of his dilemma because the God of Israel and

Judah was wholly unequal to the contest if the Gods of Assyria were pitted against him.

3. Hezekiah took the letter and spread it open before the Lord in the temple, in sight of the people and said in words that meant that it was very true indeed that Sennacherib had taken captive all the countries he mentioned, but that there was not one of them which had set its faith upon the true God. Every one of them believed in a god of wood or stone and a god without Intelligence, Life or Love, Therefore the fact that they had yielded to Assyria whose Gods were conceded to have the most powerful armies on their side of any Gods of these days, counted for nothing in a contest with the people of Jehovah.

4. What difference does it make what these people who believe in material powers, have accomplished against other people who believe in material powers. It is a principle of those who believe in Spirit and not in matter, that "It is not by might nor by power, but by My Spirit saith the Lord."

5. It is also a principle that "The King is not saved by the multitude or—of an host, neither the strong man by his valor." All depends upon Spirit. And nothing can withstand Spirit. The true God, said Hezekiah, is Spirit. He fills heaven and earth and is Lord over all Kingdoms. It is God alone who is King and none may hope to win any cause which has in it the defiance of the King of Kings and the Lord of Lords.

6. Hezekiah took the stand of every man, woman and child who believes in God as Omnipresent, Omniscient Spirit. He described the true God and asked the true God to do according to His

own way in defending Jerusalem, but to defend the city for the honor of His own cause.

7. The next morning 185,000 Assyrian soldiers lay dead on the fields and not a solitary shot had been fired from the bows of Hezekiah's army. As great a victory as history records was won by denial and affirmation. It is one of the noblest lessons of science that there need not be a single material effort made, and yet victory will be certain for those who use the spiritual efforts taught by Jesus Christ.

8. "The weapons of our warfare are not carnal, but mighty through God to the pulling down of strongholds."

9. It is true in material difficulties. It is true in financial situations. It is true in home affairs. There must be no uncertain sound in our description of our God, which is the description of our Good. Hezekiah simply told the truth about God, straight to God, and the lightning bolts of his mind struck down a whole army of those who held error. Sennacherib never attempted to fight him again.

10. How do we know how suddenly we might bring to pass the mighty works of Truth, if we should acknowledge Truth as uncompromisingly as did Hezekiah!

11. A description of matter and error as nothingness first, and a description of substance and Truth second, and you will find a wind blown forth that no masterly army could hold up under, when that army was braced up and kept going by errors.

12. What armies are now pitted against the good? You speak of poverty, sickness, pain, sorrow, hunger, cold, sin, destruction, change, decay and

many others. They are built up and moved about by error. Error is a state of the mind. Remove the error and these phantom armies must all lie motionless where they are touched by our Truth. All the mistakes of today are entirely concerning God as surely as in the days of Sennacherib and Hezekiah. And if mistaken ideas of God seem to flourish, yet they count for nothing at all under the wind of Truth set blowing.

13.   Suppose you take your life under the light of this Truth and do as Hezekiah did with his. What if sickness has blasted some of your family or even your own body in the past? Was not that body a believer in the God sickness? Why then should not matter fight matter and the side which has the most belief in it conquer?

14.   But now that you know yourself as spirit and know that spirit is God, why should you yield any longer to the great phantom?

15.   Suppose that while you believed in trials they came and seized upon you, is that any reason that now when you do not believe any longer in them, they should come near you ever again?

16.   Suppose that while you believed in the power of death, it came and took off some of your friends or family, is that any reason that now when you have pledged yourself to believe in Life only that that imaginary god, death, should have any sway with you?

17.   Suppose that while you believed in the reality of the imaginary god, matter, that you often had failure and losses and accidents is that any reason that now while the eternal Substance Spirit is your God you should ever have such a thing as failure

or loss or accident? Not at all. Your former self, yielding to all these things is not the present Self that declares them nothingness.

18. There is not the smallest item of your daily lot, but you are privileged to say: "No matter if I did claim to have such and such conditions under the reign of My imagination, which imaged a mixture of evil with My good, that is no reason why I should have such conditions now."

19. "My good is unmixed with evil of any kind. My God does not permit such conditions in his Kingdom."

20. There are five descriptions of God, which if the race make, they will send the wind of bliss and goodness over the whole earth. There are two extra descriptions of the good that belong to every man by himself, just as there are two denials of evil that belong to every one alone.

21. Moses taught the Statement of Origin in a figure. He taught the denials of science in a figure. He taught the affirmation of science in a figure.

22. "In the beginning God created," was his statement of origin.

23. "Let there be light," was his rule of denial of the void and darkness that he said compassed the mind that knew not truth.

24. "And God saw the light that it was good," was the rule of affirmations. To see is to know. To see the light is to know the Truth. To see the light that it is good, is to see that the Truth is good.

25. The description of your own idea of peace is that it shall not be mixed with disturbance. The description of your idea of love is that it shall not

be mixed with hate nor fear. The description of your idea of God is that it shall have no mixture of evil. You would choose unalloyed prosperity. The description of unmixed good with the simple request that it manifest itself, was all that Hezekiah did after declaring the nothingness of any power of presence except his God. This is where the denials of science leave us. We must see the Light that it is good. Or we must see that Truth is good and delight in it.

26. The Truth of God will work all the changes against evil that we could imagine out to be worked. If a hand is lifted to strike a helpless child or animal, would you like to see it drop and a kind action put in its place? This is exactly what happens when truth is told. If a corporation should form to close down upon the rights of the people would you not like to see it defeated without turmoil or bloodshed? There is nothing out of the power of Truth. Therefore you see the Truth that it is good.

27. The Truth of God is what the world is waiting to have spoken. The five affirmations are the Truth of God that would revolutionize the world. They come naturally and reasonably forth from you when you have boldly declared the denials of science. It is pure logic to have universal negation precede universal affirmation, both springing from a reasonable promise.

28. Rene Descartes, a French philosopher, was very learned in school matters, but he found that it all counted for nothing in the knowledge of Truth that was worthwhile. So he tried deliberately to drop out of mind what he had studied at school.

29. The knowledge of the true God is the knowledge of the motive that rules our actions. This motive is the push of the idea of good that belongs to us. When we do not express this good, there is no good manifest. When we do express this good, this good is manifest. All manifestation depends upon our expressing what we know.

30. The stars move in their eternal pathways because mind has declared for times and seasons. They will melt and disappear because mind has decreed that they shall end. "Thou shalt decree a thing and it shall be established unto thee."

31. Each man, woman and child must state for himself or for herself very definitely what he wishes to see manifest. Let there be no uncertain sound in the announcement of God. It was the uncertain descriptions of man of the past that have set nation in animosity against nation and clan against clan. They described a God who could send trouble and famine and pestilence and then lift people out of these things. They described a Being capable of intense cruelties and unreliable mercies. These descriptions, what could they bring but contrary conditions of earth life?

32. Now with our new and unmixed description of God, the new and unalloyed earth must be made manifest.

33. My God is Omnipresent, Omnipotent, Omniscient Good. My God is Life filling earth and sky and stars beyond stars. There is no point of space or place that My God with His Life unchecked, unhindered, is not eternally present. My life is God, filling all the pathways of the universe. Nothing can take away Life as nothing can take away God. Let

Life now be manifest everywhere and in everything, according to this Truth. All is Life Omnipresent, Omnipotent, Omniscient.

34. My God is Truth. Truth fills all places and spaces and atoms and objects and thoughts of Omnipresence. All things are filled with Truth and tell Truth only. To know this is to love them for the Truth's sake. Truth is Christ. Thus you know why we are to love all things for Christ's sake. Truth is good. Truth is Light that mind sees as good. Truth is the Light that shines when the true God is named.

35. Whenever the words are shed abroad that Truth is All, as God is All, error falls away forever. Truth spoken is prophesied to be the Light that shall cause the light of the sun to be no more needed forevermore, neither for brightness shall the moon give light unto the earth. Only the Lord God and the Lamb shall be the Light of the nations.

36. In the oldest religious philosophy of the world it is written, "Truth is Lord of all. There is nothing higher than Truth."

37. Only the good is truth. Whatever is not good is not Truth. And it is by the Truth of God that the good shall come manifest as Hezekiah's description of God brought him victory. Truth is victorious. Error falls under the Truth as the Assyrians fell under Hezekiah.

Omnipresent Omnipotent Omniscient

All things being now in Spirit, we do not need to
think of time in connection with the Works of
Spirit. It is promised that while they are speaking,
I will answer them.

*"And it shall come to pass that before they call, I will
answer; and while they are yet speaking, I will hear!"*
[Isaiah 25:24]

LESSON FOUR

True Relation With Your Own Eternal Self and Practice of It

1. Love is God. God is Omnipresent. Thus Love is Omnipresent. It is my idea of Good that All is Love.

2. Whoever has forgotten or neglected to call everything Love, has forgotten and neglected to speak that Truth of God whose breath is warmth for the beggars on the cold streets and food for the cry of hunger.

3. The Truth of Love is the Truth of God. The rich will share their bounty with all freely, and the poor will show honor in receiving and dealing with all that comes to them as gifts of kindness, when their animosities are melted under the hot sunlight of the Truth of Love sent over them, as the Truth of God's power being told by Hezekiah caused the Assyrians to fall by thousands.

4. Had he told the full Truth of God, the love in each heart would have melted the hate and 185,000 hearts of love would have brought mercy and good gifts into the City of Jerusalem.

5.   Spread your cause before Love and tell Love that It is God, and fills heaven and earth and is Lord and Governor of all things. Ask Love to show, for its own sake, how by its own ways, it can win your cause and do good to all people and all things.

6.   Many have suffered from lack of Love, as many Kings had been defeated because they did not describe Love. They did not talk of Love as God. The Truth of Love must be told as the Truth of God must be told. If the Truth told of Love is Omnipotence moving, I will speak truth of Love till Love plead My cause with the hunger and misery of earth, those armies that threaten the triumph of Love. 'There is none like Thee, Love of God. Thou only. None shall meet Thee to oppose Thee. Thou, for Thine own sake, work now our miracle for us."

7.   Love has conquered pain and tribulation by the Truth of God. A miracle is easy to have, because a miracle is easy to God. God is Love. Our highest Good is Love.

8. God is the only Substance. This is the Truth of God, waiting to be told.

9.   Omnipresence is the only Presence. Omnipresence is God. God is Spirit. There is no other Presence except Spirit. The Truth of God as Spirit brings the might of Spirit into sight.

10.   "Is anything too hard for Me?" saith the Lord. Spirit is not to be conquered. There is no taunt can reach Spirit.

11.   It is Spirit that makes health show. It is Spirit that makes greatness visible. It is Spirit that makes Prosperity. Spirit is the substance of all things. Spirit is the Life of all things. The Truth of

God as Spirit told, will cause the beauty of holiness to shine forth and the sweetness and goodness of all things to smile in our faces.

12.   It is Spirit that gives you your money.   It is Spirit that gives you your friends. It is Spirit that gives you your children. It is Spirit that fights your cause for you when all are opposed to you and would gladly see you fail. Some Truth of Spirit told boldly, has come from the speaker over to where your cause needed espousing, and laid all the elements of failure low like a host of phantoms.

13.   All the mysterious uplifting of men and the successes of nations are wrought by Spirit. Lay all your cause open before the Spirit. Tell Spirit that there is no failure for Her. Tell Spirit that it is in Her that you put your trust.

14.   Spirit is the Comforter. Spirit is the Holy Ghost. Spirit is the Shekinah of God. Spirit is the power of God, is the bounty of God. Spirit is the substance of God.

15.   If we think to destroy Spirit, we think to destroy God. If we speak of the breaking of Spirit, we speak of the breaking of God. And can God be broken? It was Spirit that formed all the trees and the grasses, the rocks and the seas, before they appeared in the earth. So even to destroy these things in substance, cannot be done, though we may have pulled them up by the roots and burned them in the fires to finest ashes. Still they are living in the Spirit and may spring forth any instant, young and strong and vigorous. All things being now in the Spirit, we do not need to think of time in connection with the works of the Spirit. It is

promised, "while they are yet speaking, I will answer them."

16. There is nothing you can describe of miracle working, but that Spirit is ready and able to do now. At a single description from you to Spirit, you are able to see peace, plenty and happiness everywhere.

17. "My word that goeth forth out of my mouth shall prosper in the thing which I please."

18. You are Spirit. All is Spirit. Your word is the word of Spirit. Spirit is that good that you love. Spirit is the substance which, filling your thoughts, you will see fills your heart with satisfaction. All is Spirit.

19. My good is Intelligence now speaking. I cannot speak of My God as lacking Intelligence. I cannot admit that there could be any absence of Intelligence in your world or in My world. This is the name of God, Intelligence. As God is Omnipresence, so Intelligence fills all things and all places. There is nothing but what is alive with Intelligence. If you would see Intelligence stir the mind of the stupid, you must let your Intelligence speak boldly describing the Intelligence, Omnipresent.

20. These are the words that the mind speaks according to its own orderly working after it has insisted that there could not be a mixture of evil with good and have good satisfactory. It is natural to describe what good, is when one has insisted what good is not.

21. Hezekiah followed this law by an instinct of mind when pleading for the highest good to be shown forth. He saw that the strength of Jehovah if it filled heaven and earth could not be beaten by

phantoms. So he announced boldly that his good was the power and might of Jehovah filling heaven and earth against which nothing could fight. By this bold and uncompromising description of God as Power and the sudden demonstration of strength and power, we have the hint to our own demonstrations. We must notice that perfect description of the highest good. That is God. The simple description of the highest good is the surest way to demonstrate good. The full description of God will demonstrate God.

22.   This is the full description of God: God is Life, Truth, Love, Substance, Intelligence, Omnipresence, Omnipotence, Omniscience. That which we describe as God is our idea of God. We are our own ideas of all things.

23.   The second affirmation of science is: "I am My own idea of God, and by My idea of God I live and move and have My being" This affirmation has been spoken this way: "I am the idea of God and in God I live and move and have My being." This is really more like Hezekiah's manner of speaking and is like most people's on the earth in that it puts God outside of us and projects us this way from God.

24.   But if God, the Good, is the Omnipresence, what difference does it make whether the God Intelligence that moves and fills us announces to the Intelligence without and about us that It is one with us or whether we are one with it. There is only One. That is really the strongest Truth we can tell. As Paul said, "There is one God above you all and through you all and in you all." An idea may fill the mind. An idea of God fills your mind and an idea fills the mind of God. As there is nothing for you to

be but the same Substance that God is, it is safe for you to say for your affirmation concerning yourself: "I am My own idea of God and I live and move and have My being according to My idea of God."

25.   You will notice that it is impossible for the mind to describe God, and declare honestly that its good is its God without inquiring next about its own self. So you must speak definitely of yourself in your affirmations as you must speak definitely of good or God.

26.   The I AM is very important. The I AM is Itself the relation to God. Often this I AM speaks boldly, as though the prophets. I AM GOD! It has been found to work wonders with some gentle timid people, to let the Spirit within them announce to the Heaven without them its governorship.

27.   This affirmation is the fulfillment of that prophesy in Revelations, where the temple of God is opened in Heaven and the ark is seen within the temple whereon is written the testament or covenant of God with the heart. For the temple is the mind, the ark is the heart, and the testament is the word of God. Heaven is the harmony all about us which we are sure to realize, when we open our mind to speak what is written in the heart. All that the heart can name as good it must speak boldly forth. Then the heaven around will be plainly visible. Heaven is harmony. Heaven is around us. We are the temple of God.

28.   Each heart that announces itself as its own idea of Good, becomes a living demonstration of Good. There is a kindness and strength and buoyancy about the atmosphere of one who realizes

himself as his own idea of Good, for see how noble everybody's idea of Good is! The beggar has the same idea of Good the prince has. All ask for peace, life, joy, love, justice, fearlessness, prosperity.

29. When the temple of their mind opens to disclose the heart, the golden rays stream into the heaven without and this makes such an atmosphere around, that people are healed by them.

30. If the only substance is Spirit, do you wonder that the third affirmation of your mind is: "I am Spirit-Mind like God, and reflect wisdom, strength, holiness." To reflect is to shed abroad. To reflect a thought is to send it forth. When you sit still thinking, you are reflecting. If you are sure your Substance is Spirit-Mind, you will have a buoyant and joyous effect upon all people. Their weight of feeling and their bodily notion will fall away. An idea in the mind carries its own radiance. Wherever your thought streams there is light. If you are strong in thinking: "I am Spirit—mind—like God, and reflect wisdom, strength, holiness," then the stream of wisdom that precedes forth from you, will be strong enough to lighten the mind greatly wherever it goes.

31. The stream that proceeds forth from you will be buoyant and strong and people will feel that strength. They will feel a great longing to do right when they catch your knowledge of holiness going forth.

32. There is another affirmation of ourselves that springs naturally to the lips when we are obeying the true impulse to speak highest Truth concerning ourselves. It is: "God works through

Me to will and to do that which ought to be done by Me." Be sure that this is true. It is a great rest to think how many unnecessary things we have been doing that now we are relieved from doing.

33.   God who worketh to will and to do never makes us do things impossible or exceedingly diffi-cult. "My yoke is easy and My burden is light." It is a false belief to suppose that you were made for hard work. It has been hard for people to have the idea that it was expected of them that they would wear themselves down sick or completely ex-hausted over anything in all the world.

34.   God never wearies. God never works hard. "He doeth all things well." Nothing evil must be laid to Him. It is a great mistake to think He took away the Life of anybody. Therefore your ministry is the giving forth of that life that fills you. It is the giving forth of that wisdom that fills you. The giving forth is easy. It must not be made hard. If you make it hard, stop and think: "God works through Me to will and to do that which ought to be done by Me."

35.   Then if you are sitting by a sick bed you will love to sit there. If you are presented with a heavy duty, it will seem nothing to you. God does all things perfectly and easily with you and through you and by you and for you.

36.   The fifth affirmation which seems to unite us with the Origin of all things or the Good that causes every movement is: "I am governed by the law of My God and cannot sin, cannot suffer for sin, nor fear sin, sickness nor death."

37.   There is nothing more certain than that we are all lived, moved and thought by our own idea of God. If we have been wise enough to describe the

true God, we are sure to demonstrate that we cannot be persuaded to sin, that we cannot fear that any one will ever do us any wrong and that there is no such thing as our fearing sin, sickness or death, for they are never to be in our life.

38.   Fearlessness is one sign that we have the right idea of God. To all the world announce your idea of God. If it is exactly true, nobody can be afraid in your presence, nobody can be sick, nobody can die, nobody can do wrong.

39.   Therefore, it is well to acknowledge yourself as governed by your own God, who never permits you to sin and who never lets sin, sickness or death into your world. It is the right of every creature of life to be free from sin, sickness, death. They are but phantoms, pure mockery, and it is not necessary to deal with them at all. So it is wise for the whole planet to be taught to speak the five affirmations of science.

40.   As there were seven devils cast out of Mary Magdalene, seven spirits cast out of the man's house, and seven washings for Naaman, so there are seven denials or seven rejections of what is not true. There are five denials for the societal mind and two for the particular mind. We must learn our own special denials. There are seven affirmations to fill the mind with delight when its old thoughts are gone. The five societal affirmations you know. They will lift you, in common with the world, out of the reach of the phantoms of evil and fold you round with Light. They are Good. The mind sees that Truth is good. This is Light.

41.   This is what Moses means by seeing the Light that it is Good. There are two affirmations of

Good that it would be wise for you to find and feed your mind with. They will give you new life and new health and new joy. Nobody can tell you what your two special affirmations are. But you may be sure that whenever anybody speaks anything that sounds like them, or carries an atmosphere that is like them, you will feel happier and more satisfied. Edward Irving put his hand on the head of a dying boy and said, "God loves you." The boy got well at once. Edward Irving had touched one of the boy's special affirmations.

42.   So you will find that a certain mind is helped by saying, "I am Love" while another must say, "I am beloved." It was Mary sitting at the feet of Jesus taking life easily who had the affirmation well in mind, "I am beloved." It was Martha, taking life hard, who felt the forceful words, "I am love."

43.   Those of you who have a hard lot will be rested by taking a passive affirmation like, "I am thought," instead of, "I am the thinker," because the passive idea being sent forth, borne like a ray of light on the buoyant ether, will rest you.

44.   Those who are inclined to inaction and sloth, will be made brilliant and efficient by positive affirmations like, "I am Spirit, I am Omnipotent Spirit," "I am almighty Love" and all the rest of the "I AM's." It has been very good for resentful people to say: "I am the friend of everybody and everything, and I forgive everybody and everything."

45.   "I am protected." is a good word for a timid mind to hold. "I am filled with joy and peace and buoyance and they radiate forth through Me," is a good one for a sorrowfully inclined mind to hold. It is certain that heaven lies around us and that all except joy and entrancing delight is phantom.

46.   It has been said that all our movements and operations among men and with nature are movements and operations of the dreaming of the universal mind. Be that as it may, we know that it is not possible for us to agree with the Truth of God, until we see the truth of Good. To see the Good is to love and be loved by all things.

47.   Look steadfastly into the substance of all things. Their Substance is God.

48.   There is a Principle involved in the idea of seeing things as they are. It is possible to look at anything steadfastly enough, to look its imperfections quite away and see it good. The Germans used to have a way of healing by looking straight at their patients' maladies and saying, "God looks you quite away."   It was their own Spirit looking straight past the appearance, to the true Substance of the man or woman.

49.   Then the true Substance or the true Spirit bore witness with their Spirit to the Truth of Life.

50.   The shadow of that truth is error. Error makes disease seem real. It is not real, however. You can see through disease by looking steadily through it, exactly as you can see through the Northern Lights to the stars beyond.

51.   There is really no obstacle to success. There is really no obstacle to health. There is really no obstacle to life. All that seems to be obstacle is mirage. Look steadfastly through it.

52.   The Good without and the God within are One and Inseparable. Whatever we say of our God is both without and within us, exactly as we describe it when we describe Truth. If you say, "My

Good is Life eternal," then you must know that Life is both within and without you. There is only One.

53.   Perhaps I might say that the whole of Spiritual Science is summed up in the word unity, the Unity of God, the acknowledgment that the "I am Spirit" is the only Spirit, the acknowledgment that the I am Life is the only Life.

54.   All acknowledgement of what your Good is, is called affirmation for seeing Truth.

55.   The five affirmations ought to be held by you, some one day in the week, all day. Add your own two affirmations while you are giving the five that are in the societal mind.

56. First:

My Good is my God, Omnipresent, Omnipotent, Omniscient.   My Good is my Life.   My Good is my Truth. My Good is my Love. My Good is my substance.

57.   Second:

I am my own idea of God and according to my idea of God, I live, move and have my being.

58.   Third:

I am Spirit-Mind, like my God, and I reflect Wisdom, Strength, Holiness.

59.   Fourth:

My God works through me to will and to do whatever ought to be done by me.

60.   Fifth:

I am governed by my God and cannot sin, cannot suffer for sin, nor fear sin, sickness or death.

61.   I am beloved.

62. I am at peace with all the world.

63. Bear these words in mind. There is no balm from Gilead that can heal you of sorrow like these words can heal. There is no light like the Light they can bring.

The constant thinking of Truth brightens and glorifies the body. Each part of the body illuminates and glistens with Spiritual radiance and beauty. This it does more and more until the whole body is transparent as crystal and shining like the sun.

"Let the waters be gathered together in one place and let the dry land appear." [Genesis 1:9]

LESSON FIVE

Necessity of Thinking in the Spirit

1. The mind proceeds as logically on its way of stating a truth as an apple tree proceeds from grafting to fruitage.

2. If the true words of Science have not been spoken, it is as though we were NOT. There is no such thing as not being. So it is nothing at all to our disadvantage or advantage when we are not speaking Truth. There is in reality no advantage or disadvantage. All that seems to be advantage or disadvantage is but the naming of what would be, if God were not All.

3. In Dante's "Divine Comedy," we are told, as a lofty truth, that God is really above virtue and goodness. The idea of virtue supposes the idea of wrongdoing. The idea of goodness is the hint of non-goodness. The very idea of good hints at evil. Therefore the highest statement of God that we can make is that God is above virtue and goodness.

4. Moses said, "Let the waters be gathered together into one place, and let the dry land appear." This is a figurative expression. It is like the teach-

ings of Jesus, likening the Kingdom of Heaven to measures of meal and leaven. There is a metaphysical meaning underlying the surface words. The dry land and water had nothing to do with the teachings of Moses, except to figure his metaphysical meaning. Of course the land and water of the earth do proceed into their places at the word of mind. But it is the mental experience Moses refers to, as it is the mental experience Jesus always refers to.

5.   The mental experience which dry land and water signify, is the unconscious or subconscious mind and the conscious mind. As Mind is God, the true Mind cannot be conscious or unconscious. What then do we mean by conscious and unconscious mind? We mean that we think purposely and actively as the waters flow and ebb. We mean that we forget what we have thought and yet that it is all stored within us bringing forth our affairs just as the dry land is built and formed by the waters and brings forth trees and corn. The conscious thinking makes your blood. The unconscious thinking forms your body. To change the blood changes the whole body at once. We change the blood by changing our thinking. We ought to change our thinking at once if there is anything wrong with our blood or our bones.

6.   In Edward Stanton's book he tells of meeting one named Cecil, who, though ninety years old, appears only fifty. He explains that he did it all by thinking upon spiritual themes. There is perfect health in thinking along spiritual lines. All other thinking leads to sickness and death. To be thinking spiritually is to be thinking truthfully. To be thinking truthfully is to be making the blood

strong and vigorous. Then the flesh and nerves and bones become beautiful with health and vigor.

7.　The spiritual thinking has been going on from all eternity. We have been going counter to it in the seeming. Thus we have had the counter to health and beauty and wisdom. The instant we begin to think along spiritual lines we show it by transformed bodies. The constant thinking of Truth brightens and glorifies the body. Each particle of the body illuminates and glistens with spiritual radiance and beauty. This it does more and more until the whole body is transparent as crystal and shining like the sun.

8.　There are prophecies in the Bibles of the Persians and Egyptians, as well as our own, which tell how the Truth affects the body when the highest teachings of it are proclaimed, and also that there shall be a time when the highest Truth will be proclaimed constantly. The highest Truth is that "All is God now." Speaking this Truth is proof of it.

9.　"Without the Word was nothing made that was made." What do we mean by the Word? We mean any truth told. To tell the truth is to speak the Truth. Then this Word shows forth in healthy beautiful bodies and healthy beautiful affairs. We make our world seem real to us by our words.

10.　It is written that according to our faith so is everything unto us. There was once an African king who believed that poisons stimulated and made him healthy. So he ate of poisons of all kinds and finally he poisoned those whom he touched because he had faith in poisons as good for himself but dangerous for others.

11. It must not make any difference to you how long it takes your words to bring themselves to pass. There are numberless examples of those, who, having made any one idea the subject of their constant thinking, have become like it and have thrown the indifference of their mentality around them strongly.

12. Faith is the mystery of work. "Faith without works is dead." That is, faith is as dead as nothing, unless it accomplishes something. In fact there is no faith then, for faith always works. Some kinds of faith, coming to an end, kill themselves. They have within themselves the elements of their own destruction. As for instance, the king who believed in poisons died a miserable death and his poisons ceased from helping him or hurting anybody. His faith was put in temporary and imperfect substance. It was put in the non-substance—the nothing—so it all proved nothing.

13. You may have heard of very good practitioners who have been faithfully treating sick people, and yet they died on their hands while still under treatment. Not a single word of that treatment is lost. Somewhere they will clasp the hands of those faithful workers and thank them for so much light and warmth and healing as their words are by and by brought to pass.

14. Maybe you are thinking that it is not very encouraging to a worker to have to wait till some other clime and country for its fruits. That is, as if one should say that it was pretty hard to wait for a grain of corn to grow past the stalk and silking time and harvest, before eating the grain. And it is true that time would not be considered, if faith

were hot and fervent. Perfect faith means instantaneous demonstration.

15.   How shall faith be generated? By patience. Work is brought to pass by faith. All work of every kind is brought to pass by faith. The amount of money you possess represents your faith. The friends you have represent your faith. The clothes you have represent your faith. The body you carry around represents your faith.

16.   People of temperaments and types, not at all pleasing to you, may have more faith opened up within them than yourself and so have the very blessings your soul is asking for. There is faith enough for every one to have the full faith of God. Jesus Christ said, "Have the faith of God." The Faith of God must be all the Faith of God or it is not satisfactory at all.

17.   You can have all the Faith of God and take no faith away from your neighbor, as you can have all the Wisdom of God and take no wisdom away from your neighbor. You can have all the riches of God and take no riches away from your neighbor. There is always enough and to spare. The mere knowledge of this Principle will work out your affairs in a new and different fashion. It is a knowledge that liberates a fine white light to sift itself through you and turn and overturn all your affairs, to give free way for a new set of affairs to settle themselves.

18.   All of your affairs, as you now look at them, represent your former way of thinking. They are held together by the glue of your former ideas. Now if you withdraw that glue, what can you expect, but that your affairs will all fall to pieces to let the

new affairs, representing your new way of thinking, establish themselves.

19.　　People are often astonished, after telling that God is their health to find that their health seems to fail them. The old foundations have been knocked from under them, by saying that God is their health. Formerly they felt that air and food and doctors were their health, but now they know better, and that knowledge sloughs off the health based upon foolishness. Then their health is founded on the true basis.

20.　　People say that God is their support, and their houses and lands are taken from them very soon. This astonishes them, but their possessions, which had been founded on business deals and workings after material methods, had no foundation that was worthwhile, and the true foundation would slough off all that was procured by any process unlike itself. This sudden destruction of property after making the true statement has been noticed by metaphysicians of all classes and kinds for ages. They have been almost afraid to tell the truth about possessions on account of the swift departure of them after telling the truth.

21.　　This poverty after riches, by the sloughing off of the riches so badly founded, can all be avoided by acknowledging Jesus Christ in the mind as the Saviour from poverty and trouble. In some mysterious way the name Jesus Christ is the demonstration of Good and saves from the experiences of evil which the bare truth rushes us into. For instance, if you are speaking of God as your support be sure to add the words "according to Jesus Christ," for you remember that Jesus Christ owned all the kingdoms of the world and the riches of them. That he went about leaving his possessions to take care of themselves, was just because he knew how to increase one penny into a million, any moment he pleased.

22.　　You liberate the Principle that worked through Him to operate freely through you by clarifying your mind with faith. The name Jesus Christ does not mean the historic man only. It means the visibility of power and riches and wisdom. We make ourselves and our power visible by the Name.

23.　　As the time this Principle is speeding a certain manner of speaking through us, it is saying eternally: "I can preach the gospel through you. I can heal the sick through you. I can cast out demons by you. I can raise the dead for you. My sheep hear My voice."

24.　　This Voice is perpetually speaking through you. To hear it telling you exactly what to do is your privilege. It may be heard as audibly as the voice of a neighbor or a friend. Moses heard it when he was afraid to pass through the country of the Hittites and the Amorites and the Hivites. Abraham heard it telling him not to slay his son. Peter heard it telling him to put on his sandals and cloak. There have been many men and women to whom the voice of God has sounded with plain directions as to what to do with human experiences.

25.　　It does not do to go back on or run counter to the Principle announced by us once. Steadfastness to Principles is steadfastness to life and health. Napoleon once believed that the star of his destiny was united with that of Josephine. Then he became proud and concededly independent of her and the prosperity of his course was doomed. In the subconscious region of his mind he was a believer in the possible advantage of doing contrary to principle. This was the Satan of his mind and brought him low.

26.   Deep within the mind must be as honest a principle as upon the surface. The subconscious mind rules the destiny more than the conscious mind. The subconscious comes to the surface after a while. It draws events and people like a magnet. The saints of old draw their pains and martyrdoms upon themselves by their half conscious or subconscious thought that there was a power of God and a manner of God to bring them trouble and hardship in spite of His goodness.

27.   The reserved opinion of God finally governed their human conditions. Any reservation of opinion contrary to the spoken thought or word is the conquering of destiny in the end, so that reserved opinion of God is the Satan kept invisible. People who praise God for his goodness while in their heart, they are thinking of how often he has taken their dearest hopes away, will surely see the Satan of their secret idea come forth in misfortune. This is what is meant by conscious and unconscious mind. Moses calls it land and water of our being because the land is what brings forth the substantial things of our human lot.

28.   All this conscious and unconscious mind which thinks good and evil, imagines variety, and studies into numbers and sciences, is pure mortality, the mere hint and sign and symbol of the Spiritual Intelligence, that is the substance accompanying every living creature and every growing plant and rolling stone. The most brilliant intellect is only the sign and symbol of Intelligence.

There is nothing to it. Its reality, its substance is Spirit.

29.   The more brilliant and powerful the intellect the more quiet it must keep to let the positive claims of its central substance be seen. The man who is bold and projective in his influence among men, must become meek and receptive like a crystal sphere.

30.   The Truth of God striking into him meets the silent truth within him, and when the Spirit of Truth without and the Spirit of Truth within him meet, there is demonstration of spiritual power in wisdom, in healing power, in originality of mind, in strength of character.

31.   The Science of God has not yet manifested itself from the perfectly receptive mind turned into the projective mind. All its ministry so far has been to teach stillness of intellect and dropping of sensation. It is willing to make its ministers receptive. Its next effect will be to make them projective.

32.   The truth within your mind is the real land, and the truth without your mind is the real water. Thus in truth Moses meant: "Let the truth without your mind become visible also." All mind that thinks of stones or of mathematics, though it is thinking with great brilliancy is simply a downward shading of the truth of mind which regards all things in reality and not in symbol at all.

33.   The image in the like may be very beautiful, but it is only the symbol. So the intellect of man and the fleshly body of man may be very beautiful but they are symbolic.

34.   Jesus Christ said the knowledge of the Father gave him power to lay down his fleshly body

and pick it up at will. The Father is the Origin. Of course the substance of the shadow is its Origin. Origin always means beginning or Father. The origin of the shadow in the lake is its father in the sense of standing near and casting it by the law of reflection.

35.   When the sun is directly overhead there is no shadow.   So John the Revelator prophesied when there should be no more flesh. Jesus Christ prophesied at a time when there should be no more symbol.   We now enter that hour. We are letting the deep knowledge of God within us meet the glorious knowledge of God without us and this is the earth clear as crystal, when the thoughts of all hearts shall be revealed.

36.   To meet all misfortune with the clarifying words: "I do not believe in evil at all. I believe in the Good," will be the dropping of the symbol and the taking hold of the Reality.

37.   He who knows that Truth makes over the body and changes the fortunes, knows that there must be some bodies somewhere formed by Truth, and some fortunes without misfortunes somewhere. He who is bold enough to navigate this truthful sea, will come in contact with those beings who ministered to Jesus Christ in the wilderness and greet the joyous hosts who fought for Elisha in the mountains round about Samaria. Those beings are the united Spirit of God. They are One in Substance, One in Truth, One in Life.

38.   They seemed many to Elisha and doubtless when we see them they will seem many to us. But as all land is land and all water is water, so all Spirit is Spirit. We must let fall the idea of matter and evil, to praise Spirit and Goodness. This will

clarify our crystal sphere of mind. The Mind of God that fills us full and comes teaching us lofty truths is what Moses called the earth.

39.   The first six lessons of Spiritual Science have entirely to do with the preparation of the mind for its mighty works of preaching the Gospel, healing the sick, casting out demons and raising the dead by its own nature of goodness and fitness. Works are expected to be easy. As easy as breathing so should be all the works of goodness for us.

40.   Faith is the important move for us to make. It is the separation of ourself from the misty conglomerations of ideas that the masses of people are holding into a definite form of faith for ourselves. The faith of us is the quality and character of us. We make our own quality and character. We do not do our own works. All work is done for us by the free Spirit which pours so bountifully through us after determining what we believe.

41.   The curse of laboring for the accomplishment of good works is utterly removed by the Gospel of Jesus Christ believed in, "Labor not for the meat that perish-eth," he said. Labor not for externals. Even our healthy bodies must not be worked for. They must feel the free light sifting through them with healing in its beams. All things that have to be labored for are worthless. Salvation is free. Truth is free. Strength is free. Support is free. Defense is free. Clothing is free. Shelter is free. We do not have to labor for any of these according to the Gospel.

42.   This not having to labor for God, because God is free, is what is meant by the freedom of God.   Intelligence is free. Inspiration is free. All is

free in God. Whoever has to labor for his bread or
his clothes or his home is not living or thinking according to Spirit and therefore is not free. He has
to meet the question of what he does not believe
and what he does believe face to face.

43.   While you are working to be well or working
to be wise, you show that you have this day to
meet fairly the question of what you do and what
you do not believe. Meet it boldly. While you have
worked presented to you to do, which, if you do not
attend to, it will go undone or devolve upon somebody else to do, who should not take the added
burden, you are to do that work honorably with the
distinct understanding that it is the day when you
should stand with one foot on the sea and the
other on the land of your ideas, and declare your
faith unto God. Proclaim exactly what you do and
what you do not believe this day.

44.   Sometimes people have thought that they
ought to sit right down in the midst of dishes needing washing, and account books needing straight-
ening, and refuse to do these tasks, because to be
doing them is a sign of belief in labor. It is not
yours to demonstrate the cessation of work. It is
yours to settle your faith. Keep at your tasks till
your faith is so clear that the free spirit sifting
through it, takes the dishes out of your way and
calls another to straighten your account while you
are being used as a redeemer from death and pain.

45.   All situations are brought into view by
thoughts. All people are the embodiment of our
ideas. If we take our realm of thoughts and love
each thought with praise and blessing we shall see
only people whom we love. We shall come into

situations that we love. All is first within mind before it comes out in human experiences.

46.   All that each one sees is his own idea made visible. Each good idea has its opposite as long as we believe in opposites. You have an idea of being largely generous and just. The shadow of this idea within your own mind may be that you are, along some line, very selfish in your own feelings. So when you see a very selfish person, you may know that she is just and generous in her substance, but your feelings and selfishness are peculiarly personified in her. The washing of your own mind and thought of all selfish feelings would be her cure. We are a mental sphere. We have our nationalities within us. We have companies of ideas very much alike. These all show out in people. Thus you see that to be all right within ourselves is to be all right with the world.

47.   Some have determined to live alone and spend all their time in meditation. They have felt that they were greater benefactors to the world by such a process than they would be by living among the multitudes. They have done great good in the world, and sometime we shall realize that much of our own freedom has come from the ideas of cleansing and peace which they have shed abroad.

48.   These hermits represent certain hidden thoughts of peace and rest which we keep within us. When we realize that we have a right to face our secret ideas of peace and rest and lay hold of peace and rest as our own right, we shall come face to face with the hermits who are charging the nations with the idea of peace and rest. Really they have much to tell us. They can tell us how to keep

still and let the healing Spirit flow through us. They can tell us how to hear the voice of the Spirit.

49.   Jesus Christ says: "My sheep hear My voice."   He means that those who are in the thought with Him, in the feeling with Him, will hear the Spirit utter Itself. On rare and wonderful occasions sincere thinkers have heard the voice. It never tells anything but good. It never tells of weakness. It always tells of strength. It never tells of approaching death. It tells of how to live. It never speaks of misfortunes ahead of us. It always tells of what move to make or what business to begin or pursue, to be prosperous.

50.   Hence we are always to meet every prognostication of evil with the words: "I do not believe it. I believe only in good." Then the Spirit of Truth will breathe Her breath of light through us and we shall hear and see and understand Spirit.

51.   We can train our faith by proclaiming to every sign of trouble that we do not believe in it, until we are a sphere of certainty. Then we think thoughts along the lines of truth and bring forth delightful circumstances and charming people.

52.   People are not as they seem. They are, in truth, all glorious. We need not see them as they seem. It is for us to prepare our thoughts until Divine Beings surround us. We must say to all the world, "Ye are My people and the sheep of My pasture." "I do not believe in evil. I believe only in good." As things in present stand in the world of seeming, their foundations are error and they must fall. For instance, schools are founded on the idea of the absence of Intelligence. The idea is false and when it falls to pieces, of course, the schoolhouses will fall down. The Truth is that Intelligence is Om-

nipresent. It cannot be absent. Therefore, all words and schools should be sprung from that idea. The new schoolhouses will be marvelously different from those we see now. They will have a different purpose in their building.

53.   Shall we then tear down our schoolhouses? No, they will tear themselves down.

54.   The churches also, being founded on a false idea, will fall when the false idea is removed. This is the end of the material world and this is the reason why the material world must end. Its institutions being built on a false idea must totter when those ideas are discovered.

55.   Each truth has its opposite as long as we believe in opposites. There is really no law of opposites to the highest mind.

56.   The ancients trained themselves not to believe in opposites by taking twelve o'clock noon for an affirmation which should have no opposite to meet them.   For instance, they meant that whatever we affirm at high noon, we shall never be called upon to experience as an opposite.

57.   The usual affirmations of Science are met by experiences in life quite their opposite, as if you say, "I am governed by the law of God and cannot sin, cannot suffer for sin, nor fear sin, sickness or death." You may very likely have some very sick person in your family or some great sin happen against you to test your mental strength as able to meet such things fearlessly and efficiently. But the high noon affirmation will never face you up with a calamity or misery of any kind, because there is no shadow cast at high noon.

58. All physical things symbolize Spiritual things. But all Spiritual things being the realities, we are expected to ignore their symbols as we are expected to ignore the shadows of trees and see the trees themselves when we study or are describing trees.

59. If you have a special object in life, affirm at high noon that it is accomplished. Take out that idea of time from your affirmation. The works and objects of God are already brought to pass. As you are God in character and substance, your works are really already brought to pass.

60. Prosperity is the goal of every person on this planet. So all people should proclaim prosperity. This doctrine has the lifting of all men into equal rights and equal privileges without at all interfering with each other.

61. The subconscious thought is that evil might get us by some drift of affairs. That idea is Satan. Face that Satan up. Deeper than that fear is a hope that the drift of affairs may turn in your favor. Shake hands with the hope. It is the left wing of your swift flying. Tell it you believe in it. Hope and confidence in hope will send you flying into your own country. This believing will be the right wing to take you into sight of your prosperity.

62. Remember that there is always a hope in your deep mind that things may turn in your favor. Having confidence in that hope will cause you to see that land of prosperity where you really dwell. The Soul of you lives in a land of joy and satisfaction. Live with your Soul. You live there to your conscious mind, by hope and faith. That is, as a bird's wings cause him to see the Southland, so

your hope and faith will make you conscious of your prosperity. Have faith in your hope.

63.   Faith in your hope as being the true, will bring the fair land and water of prosperity into your sight.   The land and water of prosperity are the satisfaction and wisdom of mind. Every idea has its conscious and unconscious side, just as the idea of God being the Ruler of all things, has its hidden notion that God overrules us with trials and misfortunes sometimes.

64.   Rally the whole sphere of your mind to the idea you wish to see demonstrated. Throw the whole force of your will into the noontime affirmation. It is known that at high noon the sun casts no shadow. So it is said your affirmation will not let any shadow of itself come to disturb you with the necessity for denials. If you are sure you like prosperity, put these words out over the airs for demonstration: "I am satisfied with My abundant prosperity which from this time makes no delay in pleasing Me."

65.   The idea of time is taken out of this affirmation. The usual affirmations and denials of Science have an undercurrent of feeling that it is going to take some time to bring them to pass. Meet that Satan walking about under cover of darkness. There shall be no time mixed with your demonstration of prosperity. Time is only seeming. Words are seeds thrown into arable soil. Plant them and expect their fruits. Look instantly for the salvation. You need not speak intensely. You need not watch to see your words coming to pass. They are the mystery of growing as corn is.

66. Consider this

Thou canst not see the corn grow,
How sharp so e'er thou be.
Yet that the corn hast grown,
Thou very soon canst see.
The word now prospering know,
The fruit of every word
Time without fail will show.

67.   All words of Truth are efficient. All words of Truth work. Concentrate your thoughts into a great congregation. Address them. Tell them you are the God of your realm, the Saviour of your ideas.

68.   Each of us have our own realm of ideas. It is our kingdom. We often say of God that if we had the ordering of creation we would have more happiness in the universe. But we need not say that while some of our thoughts are low and sorrowful. All people are our own thoughts. All actions are our own thoughts. We need not say that if we were God, there should be no poverty, for it is all our own idea of poverty, which we see manifest.

69.   There are certain truths we may set down as axiomatic. Knowing these truths is quite enough. They will work with us as the sun works with the seeds after they are planted. The planting of seeds metaphysically is the stating of Truth. The hoeing of the ground is confidence in Truth. The sun shines and the rain falls according to a law. So our principles being fixed in mind and loved and trusted, it is the law that they will spring forth with healing and unchanging beneficence.

70.   Every wrong is shown to be a beautiful substance, covered with the shadow of our error, knowing Truth works in this beneficent way. Then

let it be received as a mighty Principle that we have no work to do. It is all done for us.

71.   Jesus Christ understood how to express it. "The words that I speak unto you, I speak not of Myself but the Father that dwelleth in Me, He doeth the works." This Father is the Christ Principle, the Holy Spirit, the Healing Light of the world, never ceasing from its ministry. It is easy to acknowledge this healing Presence, and acknowledging Its Presence is the sight of its ministry. To know this Principle will lead into the knowledge of all other sciences as Spiritual Science.

72.   It is easy to know mathematics after studying this Principle. The forms and formulas of mathematics were all derived from the strict lines of spiritual teachings. It is said that all the ideas of moral rectitude were derived from mathematical forms and formulas, but it is more reasonable to say that mathematics are the shadow forms of exact spiritual combinations. God formed all things out of Himself. God is Spirit, therefore the origin of mathematics is in the Spirit. A point is the simplest form in mathematics. It is the starting point in geometry.

73.   In Spirit the starting point is the statement of an irresistible Principle—the statement of an universal idea. This universal idea is, "There is good for me." This good that is for me is the point of statement of Principle in Science.

74.   The straight line is the figure symbolizing the straight line of reasoning which the mind immediately proceeds to give, whenever it leaves itself free to state what follows logically, after the first propositions. The universality of this reasoning has

proclaimed its logic.   It is the twelve lessons in Science.

75.   The triangle is a simple figure in mathematics, having its origin in the prayer of fulfillment— the first line of asking for a blessing, the second line of giving thanks for its possession, the third line of trust in the Principle or confidence in the word of naming what is your good. The triangle in mathematics is the sign of the ful-fillment of hopes. Always the sign of the triangle when you see it, is that now you should ask for a blessing, affirm its possession and have confidence in the Principle you are dealing with.

76.   The Square is the outward figure of the four proclamations of the work of the Spirit. These four works of the Spirit are: "Preaching the gospel, heal-ing the sick, casting out all manner of evil, raising the dead."

77.   Walking along the square of these procla-mations of what the Spirit is doing, will draw the circle of the gifts of Spirit around us. The free gifts of the Spirit are home, and food and clothes and friends, and all that the heart loves.

78.   The sphere is the infinite multiplication of the circle. Double and treble and a thousand fold more in this life, and the blessings keep increasing until they are recognized by us as absolute Spirit. We have here the symbols of the free gifts of God.

79.   Eye hath not seen nor ear heard, nor hath it entered into the heart of man, to conceive what are laid up for us by walking our thoughts on the lines of Truth, till the circle of the gifts of Spirit are drawn around our lives.

80.   The pyramid is the triumphant crowning of a victorious life. Each one is to be crowned by the honor of having done work peculiarly his own.

81.   By this work he is honored. It is his name as the "Divine Comedy" as Dante's crown in the world of letters, or Hayden's "Creation", his name among musicians, as Mendelssohn's "Elijah" is his name—as Handel's "Messiah*' is his crowning glory—as the "Olympian Zeus" as Elis crowns Phydias master among sculptors, or his "Pallas Athena" gave him the name of "Sculptor of the Gods." All these masterpieces have been the glory of their authors. By them, their fame among men was achieved.

82.   All these great works are but shadows, dropped down, of the Spiritual name written in our foreheads, to come out in bold letters of glory before men and angels, when we hear our Lord's "well done."

83.   Because of our faithful listening at the "gates of silence" for the voice of the Holy Spirit now speaking so loudly and ready to be heard saying: "I can preach the gospel through you. I can heal the sick through you. I can cast out demons by you. I can raise the dead for you. My sheep hear My Voice."   The greatest work is listening for the voice. Its masterpiece is the translation of our mind from listening disciples to speaking apostles.

84.   There comes a time when what we have heard in the closet, we boldly proclaim from the housetop. But it is not something which we force ourselves to do.

The sudden gleams through the windows of the house of imagination have been what has made men great. They have ceased for a single second from thinking some thought and down has fallen a beam from the understanding of God.

"Then shall Thy Light break forth as the morning and thy health shall spring forth speedily." [Isaiah 59:8]

LESSON SIX

The Gateway of Silence

1. When mind is left free to run along its natural course, it finds itself making certain reasonings unvaryingly. After the idea is brought to the consciousness that God is the idea of good held by the universal mind, the next idea follows with unvarying certainty that in our idea of good there should be no mixture of evil, no matter, nothing to hate, neither sin, sickness nor death. We find that a set of affirmations of what we do think is good comes next. Then we are confronted with the necessity for choice between the former way of reasoning and the true way. This choice is the statement of faith. Then the works of faith are mentioned, as there is no faith without works. This quickens the understanding and from the moment the understanding is quickened, the creation or bringing forth of our mind is known to be the origin of all we see in the universe.

2. There is one evidence of understanding which is unmistakable. It is the love we feel in the heart for everybody and everything. It is not a question of

what they do or do not do, it is the spontaneous kindness which we feel without effort. God is Love.

3.   God does not love the murderer less than he loves the saint. The Soul always dwells in sinless beauty no matter how badly the shadow, called flesh, performs. The shadow on the wall might look as if some terrible tragedy were being enacted while the people who cast the shadows were having some innocent amusement. The flesh is the "shadow that declineth."

4.   There is another set of experiences following this fleshly manifestation, which is called the astral. If you think of the astral body you easily appreciate that it is but the ghostly shell of this human body and mind. Then come and look at all the earthly actions of mankind. They are as much ghosts and shells of the real body as the astrals are. Nothing is real but God. There is a spiritual body employing itself with the fullness of joy. It knows no pain, no grief, no effort. This spiritual body is ever in us and over us and around us.

5.   "The fashion of the world passeth away." The fashions of all the world passeth away. The changeless God continues—Soul—Spirit—Mind. All efforts to make the astrals visible are but the efforts to make other shadows manifest.

6.   There is no way to enter into understanding of that substance and action which is fullness of joy except by the doctrines and teachings of Jesus Christ. There is no doubt but that we have so far made bungling work of His teachings, but the purpose to understand Him will give us more direct arrangement of them till we are suddenly one with them. The effect of practicing the works of Jesus

Christ is the understanding of the Principle that governs them.

7. We give our mind freedom for the Spirit of Truth to pass through, and great works are accomplished by us. The sick are healed and it is no effort to us. The very dead are raised and we have made no struggle to have it so.

8. Whatever we know and whatever we accomplish comes about by our speaking and thinking Truth. The only effort along the way of mental procedure where there is the semblance of effort, is when we are called upon to choose between the error that seems so real and the Truth that is so real —the reality of Spiritual Substance and the claim of material substance.

9. We shall see that all efforts to make the race better by material processes must fail, while all the teachings of Spirit, making impressions upon the mind and bringing them out in clear relief, as the idea of mind, will succeed.

10. That which our mind holds as true, we shall see increase in our world. Mind doubles and trebles its creations by speaking of them. Everything is self-increasing. Words originate all things, and all things love to be praised for their greatness.

11. Praising their endurance will increase their endurance. It is as good as praise of drunkenness and crime to call them something great. They swell up with unreasoning pride and show themselves more gigantic than ever. All the time they are nothing. Their only manner of departure is by the disintegrating word of nothingness. Does drunkenness reason? Do not we do all the reasoning? Has crime intelligence that we watch its procedure and detail

its actions? How does crime increase except by describing its greatness? How does virtue increase except by describing its greatness.

12. Who made vice and who made virtue?

13. When the boldest thinkers along the religious lines arose in the past, they left gradually the notion of a great creator sitting on some majestic throne at a great distance from mankind. They have from first to last without exception, agreed with Jesus Christ that the Creative Principle was within themselves. "The Father and I are One." Father means Origin—First Cause—Creator—Creative Principle.

14. The Oriental poets have been bold in their religious proclamations in these later years. The writer of the *Bhagavad Gita,* an Eastern Bible, would have been executed if he had let mankind read his book, while he was yet manifest in the flesh. He was given wisdom enough to write that the mind of man and the mind that is God is One, and then to leave the writings to posterity to pronounce upon, as the direct revelation of Brahman to man. Brahman was his name for God.

15. One of their inspired poets, Omar Khayyam, found his soul liberated to fly through the universe. He would not be reconciled to any mode of redemption from evil, related by any religion having reign upon the earth. He was sincere and fearless. Sincerity is within itself the faculty of discovery. Sincere investigation will discover the issues along any line it pleases to set out upon.

16. Omar Khayyam reports this way:

"I sent my Soul through the Invisible,

Some letter of that After-life to spell:

And by and by my Soul returned to me,

And answered, "I myself am Heaven and Hell."

17.   To understand that here at this center the "I Am" of us is one God, with power to increase crime by calling it great, with power to increase virtue by calling it great, is to know that this profound oriental voice, Omar Khayyam, speaks truth. Cannot I start forth and describe anything to be great which I please? Cannot I agree with Jonathan Edwards and formulate a hell if I please? Will I not stand face to face with this place of my own creation? May I not experience that which I project? This brings us to where we are able to see that if we increase a crime by describing it, and increase a virtue by describing it, that neither of these is real, only as we give it reality.   This leaves as the only indestructible Reality, this center whose name is I. This center whose name is I may call Itself "I Am." It may call Itself "I will." It may call itself by any name it pleases. It may describe any scene it pleases. It may experience any ecstasy or pain it pleases.

18.   This knowledge makes every mind that catches it, ready to cease from thinking. This ceasing from thinking is the end of the world. And this ceasing from thinking is the silence in heaven for the space of half an hour. From this mighty science, mind rises and recreates its world.

19.   As the mind that has thought the fallacy that nine and one equal eleven, drops that sum when it speaks ten, so the mind that has thought evil and matter drops the fallacy when it speaks Truth. What that Truth is, which mind shall speak after its true silence, not one has spoken. So the

true creation is not seen by any. Thus the gateway of silence is the first truth of creation.

20. This law of first speaking forth Truth from the heart of silence, has been practiced by the mystics without demonstration. Therefore they have not truly ceased from thinking. To cease from thinking while purposely determining that certain things are true, is not silence. The Eastern mystics ceased from thinking, while firmly convinced of caste. The Western thinker ceases from thinking while firmly resolved upon the recognition of mankind.

21. To cease from thinking, resolved upon nothing, is the true silence. Here at the true point of silence, is the hot glory of understanding. Walled in by no more resolutions, this understanding flashes its beams to the immortal distances of the horizons of God. It is by understanding that the heavens are formed. It is by understanding that the earth is peopled. All things change by the use of understanding.

22. The sudden gleams through the windows of the house of imagination have been what has made men great. They have ceased for a single second from thinking some thought and down has fallen a beam from the understanding of God. Then their actions have been noted among men. Success has crowned their efforts while yet they made no effort. God makes no effort. He who makes effort a struggle, is not shedding abroad the light of understanding.

23. "God saw that it was good." God sees. Understanding sees. Its seeing is its fulfillment. All aspiration stops the instant one sees, for aspiration is hoping to see, while seeing is satisfaction.

Does God hope for something to come? God hopes for nothing because God understands all things, how they are made. That which we understand, is easy for us to do.

24.   Michelangelo could see in a rough block of marble the face of an angel of beauty. It was easy for him to keep his mind on the angel and let his hands perform mechanically the task of cutting the figure out of the solid rock.

25.   An architect sees the cathedral in the quarry. No obstacle daunts him. It grows out of his lofty ideal easily. To those who have not had this beam from the sunshine of understanding flash down through their minds, all work looks hard. Exertion seems written all over the success in their prosperity. There is a way to let some one thought cease from going forth which would make a space or opening, through which might stream a beam from the understanding of God, and then the way to their own prosperity would seem the most enchanting pathway over which they could walk.

26.   To one who is not rested in the satisfaction of certainty that he has all the prosperity he cares for, it is well to sit down and take notice, which of the ideas of the world holds him in its clutches, then let that idea fall as a mantle from his shoulders. With the fall of that idea is made a vacuum through which may stream the light of understanding.

27.   If a man has taken on the whole world's idea of severity, as the Czar of Russia, for instance, let him take pains to drop his severity. Let him drop his idea of what is just, his idea of reward and punishment, his idea of governing anybody or any-

thing, even his own bodily movements. Let him cease absolutely from dictation. At a certain point of ceasing from government, he will suddenly understand his own pathway to greatness.

28. If one has taken on the kindly temper of the world, he is often disappointed with the usage people make of him by taking advantage of his kindness. So shall he cease from thinking of there being any people in need or people with pleasant countenances. He shall cease from thinking of there being any people at all. He shall cease from admiring the beauty of the skies or the earth. He shall cease from thinking of the goodness of God. At some stage of such ceasing there will be a wonderful opening made for a beam of the understanding of God to pour down through him a light to show him his own line of prosperity.

29. Prosperity means success in some line of endeavor pleasing to the mind.

30. The artist never hates his work. He finds an ever-increasing beauty in the increasing beauty of his ideal. His pictures, his sculptures, show forth greater and greater possibilities. Alone with his ideal, he is alone with the ray of light streaming down from the center of his own being where pure understanding shines. Coming at a ray of understanding by such a deliberate step is science. This understanding never leaves him.

31. Those who feel the light of the understanding of God beating hot against the gateway of their being, sometimes choose to think other thoughts just at a moment when to stop thinking would be their glory.

32.   Sometimes a man who has clothed himself with the earth idea of kindness, just at a moment when his heart is wounded by some undue use of his kindness, should keep perfectly silent. He should utterly cease from thinking. For there is a hot ray of love beating hard against the window of his being to melt for him that trouble. But he closes the window still more tightly by rehearsing to his friends or weeping within his own mind.

33.   The only safe words to use in a moment of hot feeling are the words of the "I" at the center. The "I" at the center sees all things as good. One word of the "I" at the center spoken over and over will melt the hard block at the gateway of mind. Some have found that God at the center, dwelling forever in the light of understanding, sees in Jesus Christ all his world. Jesus Christ, to the "I" at the center, dwelling in the ineffable Light of understanding, is not only the man of history, but the heaven and glory Jesus preached. There is more in the name Jesus Christ, to the mind gleaming and shining with Understanding, than to the mind that speaks the name as an echo from one who only felt a trifle of the heat of the white light of love. God is Love. God is Understanding.

34.   Wisdom is within him that has understanding and they that understand among the people shall be "wise and do exploits" [Daniel 11:32]. "Exploits" are prosperous words. "Wisdom" is Understanding.

35.   The mind that has taken the five words of Science sincerely, finds at his sixth experience, a light breaking over his mind from the center of his being and the questions that looked unanswerable are now clear in his mind. The sight of a man in

perfect health is revealed to him where everybody else on the whole round earth sees miserable sickness and deformity.

36.   When we reflect that everybody on the earth represents some thought of his own, we plainly see that it is only through one window of his soul that he looks at the man. If he looked through every window of his soul, he would surely see all the world as the perfect creation, Moses declares. God at the center sees.

37.   All God should beam through the mind. This is the sixth power of Truth. Its Word is, "I understand the secret of instantaneous Spiritual healing."

38.   Healing means making whole. To make whole is to see things whole. As present we see only half or some fractional part of an object.   Even the head of a pin is not visible to any set of eyes in creation. But Mind that is God, sees the whole of the universe under and over and through all. He who heals, or makes, or sees around and through his world, is the Mind of God. He understands God. He is One with the Mind that is God. The secret of God is seeing all things as good.

39.   They who see from the center where the mind that is God dwells, see nothing evil because they see it in its entirety. The beggar, seen through and over and around, is the glory of God. The murderer, seen through and over and around, is Jesus Christ. The privilege of mind is to see as God sees. This is being One with God. This is atonement. Jesus Christ made atonement. He stopped thinking and began to speak straight from the center with God. Then he saw all as good. He saw no leprosy. He saw no thief on the cross. He saw no adult-

adulteress. He saw no murderer. He saw glory at all times. His way of meeting all the afflictions and trials and hardships of the mind was by right words. He saw all things as the product of thoughts. He saw that when truth is not spoken, evil will seem to be spoken, so long as man does not know the meaning of silence. There is no silence of Truth. Truth speaks within itself at the center of Being.

40. When error is silenced, the voice of Truth is heard through the mind. Its voice is clear and distinct. It sounds to the man who has kept silent telling him what to do, as plainly as the voice of a friend. And it never speaks to him with a message he would feel was too hard to carry out in daily life. It has spoken to the sincere mind of the doctor of herbs, telling him what herb to use. It has told the businessman what line of action to pursue. It is the guide of each mind on the plane where he is thinking. All It asks is that mind keep silent as to error, and open-eared to Truth.

41. All books which are termed inspired, were written by those whose mind was letting fall some material idea, when through the rift, the understanding of God idea was dropped leaving them their direction as to what to write. Truth is always good. It is always kind. It always intends you happiness. Yet it will answer your prayers exactly.

42. If your mind is censorious through reflecting the censorious side of the mind of each man in the race, and you pray for success, you may be increased in censorious-ness, until you are a perfect success at that. Having let that characteristic reign over you, the idea of perfecting it may be the unconscious notion of success that stirs you, so you

would be perfect success at that characteristic while you were wishing for success in health or freedom from sorrow.

43.   Make the idea of success course its way through the lines you choose. Make your choice of what your success is to be and name it prosperity. There are no evil lines with the Spirit. To mankind there seem to be evil lines, but to the Spirit there is no evil.

44.   We make lines of distinction because we do not see as Spirit sees. We speak ill of people and things but they are all good to the Spirit. When we are trying to see as Spirit sees, we call it love. There is no unworthy object to Spirit. There is no crime to the mind in understanding. The lines of unworthiness are all made by ourselves. We have covered ourselves over with the tattoo marks of distinction and difference. Hence we have to open the particular window we wish to see our success through.

45.   Men sometimes say that to have much gold is to be materially minded. But it is no more material even when one hoards it up, than to be open-hearted and generous to beggary. Both are evidences of being closed on the side of the riches of God. He who knows the mind of God can fill his hands and empty them by his words. He can lay down his life and pick it up. He is full of the power and understanding. He is never heard criticizing anybody. He has no criticism in his mind. He is free minded. There is no greater evidence of understanding than love of all things. It can manifest power as no other line of character can. Yet love that is only caught as a trick from the societal mind is not secure any more than hate is secure.

The love of understanding is the love that shines out from the center through the chinks made by dropping the former thoughts.

46.   There have been many thousands of ways of communicating this lesson with the idea of having the understanding of God break through all our being with light. God is light. Light is Understanding. To understand anything so as to have power to work with it, is some hint of the light of God breaking through. The light of God, here at the center of Being, should break through every transaction. "Then shall thy light break forth as the morning and thy health spring forth speedily," saith the Scriptures.   Health is wholeness. "Be whole," said Jesus.

47.   The three wise men fell into the fire because they saw success through fires. Fires are cleansings. Cleansings are denials. When ideas are dropped there is freedom from them. If a mind has held an idea of material and fleshly sickness or swelling deformity, it may be that it will only drop that idea by some notion of burning as they burn out cancers. Maybe the mind can only get free by harsh usage. But these are modes of cleansing— one idea counteracting another. No process of getting free is reliable except through the wisdom of understanding. Understanding is peace. With Me is peace. Understanding is strength. I Am strength. Understanding is joy. With Me is fullness of joy. Understanding is the ability to do all things. "There is nothing too hard for Me."

48.   The mind that is bright with the glory of understanding finds Heaven here. It looks forward to the continuance of Heaven forever. It looks back upon Heaven as its Origin. The past of the mind is

understanding of God as God. I am Alpha. The future of the mind is the understanding of God as God. I am Omega. All is good to the mind in the understanding of God.

49.   The good that mind knew was for its use and delight, it now sees in its daily life. The fullness of satisfaction melts the material universe down to the Substance of Spirit. To understand God is to be God. To understand Love is to be Love. They who wrote the Scriptures had gleams of the wonders of Reality that annulled the sight of the material universe. There was none in their sight. "The earth is clean dissolved," said one. "The end of all flesh is come before Me," said another. "In Thy light shall we see Light," said a third.

50.   Understanding is Light. Having understanding we know that all is good. We do not have to study to know. We do not have to ask questions. We know.

51. Here at the center with the hot fires of God, we melt down and forget the former things. The new heaven and the new earth of Divine Prophecy break into view, and with us as with Jesus Christ, "It is not robbery to know that we are God."

Omnipresent Omnipotent Omniscient

There are not multiples of beings. There is only One, There is nobody hungry for us to serve him. There is only One to serve. That One is satisfied already. To hold this porthole open for the radiance of Divinity to pour through is to be strong to bear up the race of men in our arms while we wash them from all past thoughts.

"Let the earth bring forth grass and herb yielding seed, and the fruit tree yielding fruit after its kind, whose seed is in itself, upon the earth" [Genesis 1:11]

LESSON SEVEN

Bringing Forth the Fruits of the Spirit

1.   After understanding of principle, the mind naturally begins to bring forth works something like the understanding.

2.   All the first chapter of Genesis pertains to mind with its way of coming forth from the deeps of invisibility to the most perfect manifestation.

3.   Mind, as a whole, seems to be utter void and chaos until it moves with the word of truth. Then it quickens and brightens until it is absorbed in truth and gives forth truth continually. It is a very good sign of the quickening of truth through our mental planet or earth when we are not miserable or happy by the things of matter or flesh.

4.   It is possible to be so delighted in pure truth that we do not notice anything which formerly pleased or displeased us. Our earth is just alive enough with understanding to spend all its energies bringing forth the fruits of the Spirit.

5. The fruits of Truth are the fruits of the Spirit. These fruits are happy, healthy feelings, which when being radiated from us, the inhabitants of

the world among whom we walk, catch them and are made happier and healthier by our presence.

6.   We may do this consciously or unconsciously. We do bring forth qualities which transform people by simply knowing that our thoughts are true.   But it is noticeably certain that Jesus Christ was supremely conscious of what he was doing and that Moses, by making the idea of bringing forth our fruits follow spiritual understanding, must mean that perfection of mind fruitage is conscious power.

7.   A true feeling in the mind will cause a heart to renew its hope. The renewal of hope in the heart will cause a tree to bud and backward grass to spring up. There are multitudes of springing forth which a truly right feeling of joy will cause.

8.   These lessons of Moses and Jesus are in no sense suited to a mind that feigns an interest in spiritual themes. They are suited only to a mind quickened by genuine love of God, the Spirit.

9.   The swan came swinging down to tell the heron of the fair skies and lofty hills, the balmy airs and tinkling brooks of another realm.

10.   "Are there any snails there?" asked the heron. Thus a mind entranced by truth and full of sweet enthusiasm speaks of the splendors of spirit, the gladness of Omnipotence to one whose chief thought has been, How shall I get My feet straight?" or "How shall I win the praise of the human populace?"

11.   This mind whose theme is the snails of the human flesh, looks eagerly to the things of spirit, hoping for it to set these things right. But spirit will not answer just that one prayer of the human

cry. The heron will find snails n the swan's fair realm, but the swan will never tell him that he must fly high and go gladly over the far winds before the snails will be visible. And then his taste for the old snails will be utterly gone. The swan will be rebuffed and the heron will not set forth if the truth be told him. How wisely must the mind that flies to the heights of rejection of home, of friends, of honor among the race, of all things once held dear, speak the statement of Omnipotent, Omniscient Being, deny affirm, urge faith, works, understanding, before the human heart can agree that the thing that the heart is set upon, be given up willingly.

12.   At this point of the teachings of Jesus he said: "Not my will but Thine be done." "I came not to do mine own will but the will of Him that sent Me"

13.   It is probably the one supreme test of our interest in the Truth when we feel that neither the glories of heaven nor the laws of the Spirit, presented to our consciousness by our studies or our companions in the study of the Science of God, comfort us if that one ugly unfulfilled demonstration is still in our life.

14.   Shall the obligation to give up the favor of one woman dim the peace of Truth in the heart? Shall the honor of one circle of friends, if it be lost, ruin our hopes? Shall the deformity of our back, being still in our body, waiting the adoption, to wit, the redemption, hide the mind's bliss in the contemplation of God and the kingdom of heaven? Shall the feebleness of our frame, being still holding out, keep us from chanting in daily hymnals the sweet strength of Jehovah?

15.   Now, shall these things continuing with us be signs of the Spirit? No. Here is the finest of all the fine lines over which the soul walks on the way proving its son-ship to spirit. The pains and discords of human experience are not sent of God. But they do indeed stand as tests of how much God we have. For the supreme giving up to the will that is Divine, asking nothing of the things opposite to the Divine, is quickly manifest by perfection — in some special condition of affairs peculiar only to the one who bears them.

16.   As there is one cure that stands for the acquiescence to the Science of Mind, so there is one cure that stands for the yielding in absolute submission the human tastes, ambitions, loves, longings, petitions to Divine Mind. At the point of this yielding the face is not strained with anxious longing or the disappointment of futile effort. At this point the things of home, the things of school, the things of church, the things of society, the dealings of men, women, children, do not hurt nor terrify nor distract us. At this point the Science of Moses meets us and says, "Now, heart of God alive with Truth bring forth."

17.   Out of the mind that is unspoken the spoken word comes forth. "Let the earth bring forth trees and grasses."

18.   Sweet helps to the people around us are the trees and grasses. Now it is that the Word is fruitful. The Unspoken Word of Truth is typified in the seeming or symbolic world of the appearance of void and darkness. Its coming into sight is the wind moving over the waters. All things of the symbolic or appearing world are formed by some word not truthful.   All enduring delights are

formed by truthful words. Now, it is of truthful words and their issues that we shall speak.

19.   The heart has a store of Truth all unspoken.   It breaks forth into speech and conscious thought now and then. The great white glory within, all hot with the spirit, warms some word into a feeling and a shape as the warmth and dew force the amoeba to spring into the germ of a man or a plant. That which the sunlight of understanding has gleamed over is stirred to take form. The light of Divine will is stirring the still light of the mind to determine what shall be our work in the vineyard of Jehovah.

20.   The perfect healing power sets forth when that last evidence of acceptance of Spirit is given which is the absolute yielding of the things we want to the higher way not discernible by the eyes of flesh.

21.   On the plane of sense, this is symbolized by the blind passions and appetites which stir until they yield to their law of selection and bring forth the creatures of sense. To refuse the reality of this symbol is to have a great strength come to us, to be born from us. It is as though we should uncover a force, for us to simply know that the passions and appetites of flesh are the symbol of a process of mind speaking its thoughts forth.

22.   God is the one Substance out of which all thoughts spring and are made; as protoplasm, the symbol of God, is the one Substance out of which the amoebae spring that by choice of warmth and the union of moisture make men or stones as the choice shall decree. Is protoplasm the direct symbol of God Unspoken? No. Protoplasm is the indi-

rect symbol. How is this? The direct symbol of the mind that is God is the thought of God not true— the mass of error whose place is nowhere, whose race is Adam, whose being is nothing—and protoplasm is the direct symbol of the vague error—the unreal, the untrue. All things of matter and Adam are the outward picturing of ideas not true. So matter is the sign of error: its disappearance is the approach of the sight of truth.

23.   Truth is a healing principle. For the mind that lets truth filter down through it, there is such a warm rich vegetation, such shades of delight, that the living creatures find pastures. "He leadeth Me in green pastures."

24.   Who shall let this healing, reforming, life-giving principle come strongest through him? Certainly it shall be he who has no thought of error, who is freest for Spirit to find passage through his mind, which holds up dark imaginations against the One Substance and Its creations.

25.   He shall not admit that there could be any other creation except the true thought of God. All else is but unreality. This will cause him to see all men and women as free from the claim of the senses. To him they shall be white with the falling goodness of Spirit. He shall never be heard accusing them of lustful passions and sensual appetites.

26.   The first angel of accusing shall be hushed into nothingness forever by the trained mind.

No appetites rule any creature.

There is only one Substance out of which all creations are made. That Substance is God. To see any other substance except God is to see symbol. To see evil is to see symbol. To feel unhappy is to feel symbol. To feel incapable is to feel symbol. These are not truth. They are not reality. You need not see and feel them. Yield them utterly.

27.   This will be the time for the living warmth of the loving spirit to give you the feelings and thought that make happy fulfillment of hopes.

28.   The *Dharma Sutra* is a sacred book of Buddha's sayings. He said, "Beware of the delusions of matter" Then he said, "Follow not after vanity, nor after the enjoyments of love and lust." Again he said, "He who reflects and meditates obtains an ample joy."

29.   The following after the flesh is vanity. The flesh is matter. Whoever has his heart set on things of sense, of matter, even for the order and beauty and possession thereof, is set on vanity, is set on delusion—needs to take from his mind the accusations of appetites. He has desires, not Truth. He finds a window darkly curtained through which the healing Spirit will not flow. Let him drop his curtain of desire. It is great strength to be free from desire.

30.   In the book of Revelation, the strength of the first beast is given to him who has dropped the hunger of desire for matter to please him.   One who is harassed by matter shall drop the accusation against man and woman that they want something of him.

31.   If he is tortured by the idea that they want something hard, he shall know that he is never to be able to gratify them because that is the line where the Spirit demands surrender.

32.   The curtain of desire must fall for the strength of endurance to stream through.

33.   The first beast is the symbol of withdrawing the thought that men and women or events ask something of us. They do not ask anything. They are nothing—not capable of asking anything of us. The rule of life shall be that there is nothing expected of us.

34.   The strength of endurance is the strength of long holding out against the seeming desire of the world. In the midst of their claims, he is silent who does not admit that they are making claim on his strength or his body.

35.   There are other strengths that come with other curtains dropped from the windows of soul. To drop the accusation against mankind that they have any deception of evil or sickness or sorrow will make the strength of bravery or boldness or daring. This is the second beast of strength. Its name is the strength to dare. To drop the idea of there being any semblance of power should make one bold to dare. If there is no pain, why should a martyr flinch? If there is no sickness, why should fear of sickness cringe the expectations? If there is no death, why should the speaker of truth fear the violence of armies?

36.   The third accusation being removed causes the strength of doing to come forth, the strength of efficient accomplishment of great works.

37.   In the *Bhagavad Gita,* a sacred book of the ancient Hindus, who had their religion long before the Buddhists of Buddha set forth, we are told that when one had attained to union with the Supreme Brahma, he finds all work done for him. He has the strength of works—the strength to do. This shall come when he has taken down the curtain of the idea of sin.

38. The idea of the wickedness of mankind, their sins as keeping them from being worthy of healing, from being worthy of blessings, from being worthy of life and praise, keeps the holder of such an idea from feeling the great works of God being done by him.

39. Drop the accusation of sin from the face of the world and great works will be easy. This beast of power to accomplish is the third beast of Revelation. It is the sacred strength of Jehovah.

40. The fourth accusation which the mind lets fall is the idea of speaking and action and thoughts of foolishness and ignorance. Who is there to speak and act folly? No one. The great strength of silence comes shining down with the supreme power of Omniscience when silence is held concerning the people as being foolish and ignorant. This shall not be said even in apology, or externalization of seeming folly.

> Nobody did folly. Nobody thought folly. Nobody spoke folly.

There is supreme strength in silence under the appearance of folly and nonsense.

41. Jesus Christ was speaking of the great wisdom of the Spirit, and the flesh heard him say, "Forgive them for they know not what they do." Had he not told them that they came forth from God only? Should he even on the cross forget his own words? Can the idea of there being flesh and doing folly come into the mind of Christ who never condemned anybody? "Call no man your Father upon earth, for one is your Father, even God."

42. So he was thinking of the sonship of Jehovah. He was taking his place as the only Son of

God. There is one Father, one Mother, one Off-spring. The name of that One is I AM Spirit, I AM MIND. I AM GOD. "By Me kings reign and princes decree justice."

43.   I am the creator of all my universe from the substance which I am as Good unmixed with evil. The mind which speaks in the good creation stands in the sun. John, the Revelator, knew that all the material earth should slough off and roll by like a mist from the face of the sun with the withdrawal of all accusings.

44.   The Angel of Wisdom should stand in the sun and forth from that word should spring the sight of the true heaven and the true earth. "And the former heaven and the former earth shall pass away." "They shall be forgotten, neither shall they come into mind any more."

45.   The imagination of their being an opposite substance to Spirit shall cease. "There shall be no more sea" of words and thoughts restlessly coming and going. There shall be no more death and hell. These shall be swallowed up in the victory of true thoughts.

46.   The amoeba of protoplasm shall never rear its hungry lips, for there is no thought to start him but on the face of life. The protoplasmic void shall cease to symbolize the great unspoken word of Omnipotence.

47.   The ways of desire shall cease, for where there is no accusing of desire there shall never be hunger and there shall never be stuff out of which to create hunger. The law of the Spirit is the operation to erase matter.

48. The word of the Spirit lifts man from the clutch of the hunger of his material ancestor, the amoeba of flesh.

49. Nothing projects man upon the pages of Spirit except the will of the Divine ignoring the hunger of mortality.

50. The asceticism of the ancients was the falsifying symbol of the joyous dropping of the flesh when the Divine Spirit teaches.

51. He to whom the dropping of the appetites of matter is hard, may strike back to his imagination of there being an opposite substance to Spirit out of which living things were projected. He who cares for the praise of man may drop his thoughts of amoeba, for these things are the beginning of hunger.

52. There are not multitudes of beings. There is only One. There is nobody hungry for us to serve him. There is only One to serve. That One is satisfied already.

53. To hold this porthole open for the radiance of Divinity to pour through is to be strong to bear up the race of men in our arms while we wash them from all past thoughts.

54. The hungry for bread are fed. Therefore there is no sickness or deformity from the hunger for bread.

55. The hungry for praise are satisfied. Therefore there is no deformity nor poverty. The hunger for lust and sensation is filled with the glory of God. Therefore there is no weakness nor squalor. The hunger for splendor is filled with the fiery sunshine that spreads around the Angel of Peace.

Therefore there is no paleness nor wild beast clutching for beauty and honor and the kindness of man.

56.   This is the first fruit of understanding. Only the wise through yielding their hearts desire shall know the strength of the first beast.

57.   Look into the *Bhagavad Gita* and you will see there the word of the Spirit, that it is in getting entirely free from physical objects that the ideas of Truth may be lived with entirely. All objects as they appear now are the creations of the ideas of error. Live with the ideas of Truth. To withdraw from the ideas of sense and still keep thinking the ideas of error, is the beginning of aberration. For the ideas of error will keep on formulating conditions of misery just as long as they are held in mind whether men know what they are forming or not.

58.   So the holding of one idea that is not true will soon make some hardship. To hold the idea that someone can do you any harm and wants to have you do something out of your power is a false notion which the withdrawal of mind from ideas of Truth will cause the false notions to increase and thrive.

59.   Let no error get control of the mind. Let no amoeba get started because of your false notion.

60.   The vague mass of unexpressed error which starts the protoplasm of invisible hiding between the mind of man and the mind of Jehovah is safer than the holding of some cherished terror, some definite hatred, some repelling objection. These are the opening mouths of desire. They are the hunger of the senseless passion of something shaken into

separation from out of the nameless fears of a mind in error.

61.   Never define a fear. Never speak a terror. Never let a passion to stand well in somebody's estimation get a place in your mind. Never give reign to a hatred. These thoughts are the formulations of passion and appetites.

62.   The protoplasm is not hungry. It is a symbol of the subjected will. It looks to nothing but lets Divinity have all. Will subjected is symbolized by the protoplasm that waits for the warmth and moisture to chase into form full of living energy or swing in space as worlds.

63.   The amoeba is hungry. It is full of desire. It eats and gnaws and charges to eat and gnaw until it devours its neighbors. So the idea that gets formed from the vague terror of error into the world, telling of its fears as a misery unbearable, of anguish of things to come, is hungry for new thoughts to feed upon. It puts up its mouth and gnaws out the substance and vitality of other thoughts until the mind is left a barren waste for the thriving of this one thought.

64.   This the world calls insanity. It is the lustful idea of one idea. Deny this one idea its hunger. Stop its action by one word of Truth. For though it lifts up its miserable head and seems to be strong, it is nothing. Its name is the passion of mind to have some one condition of human life changed. And human life in that one particular never shall be changed until mind steps backward into the sunlight with its Angel of Truth. One Angel of Truth will put mind backward into its beautiful

place of yielding where the first thought of Truth that springs shall be.

"I am satisfied with the bountiful goodness of God"

Omnipresent Omnipotent Omniscient

Here where the "I" of man is called the child of destiny, we proclaim every I AM to be Almighty God. There is no child save the thought of God. Where is God not his own Idea? God and His Idea are One. Is the Idea of God made of matter or is it made of his own Substance? If God is one Presence, whose name is I AM, then I am that One Presence and my world is my self-Spirit, and not matter.   I AM my own Light.

"The natural man receiveth not the things of the Spirit of God, for they are foolishness unto him and he cannot know them, for they are spiritually discerned, but he that is spiritual judgeth of all things, yet he himself is judged of no man." [I Corinthians 1:15-16]

LESSON EIGHT

The Eternal Substance

1. Science teaches that if we know the progress of one single thing on its way from its protoplasm to its fruiting time, then we know the progress of everything.

2. The protoplasm of an object is the formless stuff of which it is made. As protoplasm it looks like one simple mass of substance. It seems astonishing that out of this stuff Socrates and the white ant were formed by the same stages as the sun and the violets. This formless life stuff composing physical objects is but a symbol. It has no reality. It is the veil formed by thoughts not real.

3. Who thought the thoughts that formed the protoplasm? Nobody. How do they come floating around forming protoplasm which develops into stars and men, cattle and insects? They are the naming of what would be, if the mind that is God were not the only mind.

4. You see that there would be two forces or even more than two forces, if there were not One only. You can see that there would be many objects

and many people if there were more than One. The very fact of their being a law that would be if God were not all makes many realities. Whoever identifies himself with the unrealities puts himself into their performances, and will go from protoplasm to other experiences.

5.   The mind that for one single flash of an instant imagines anything besides God only, starts a vivid imagination, and the protoplasmic void is formulated that instant to symbolize it. To imagine still further is to run that protoplasm into a tree or a sun according to what we imagine.

6.   All things which we have imagined not based on the good are the heaven and the earth with all the inhabitants as we now observe them. Their bases is nothing. Their history is nothing. At the first trump of our high resolve to be true they shall roll up like a scroll and vanish quite away.

7.   It was the teaching of Jesus Christ that we should lay the axe at the root of our imaginations and reject the very starting point by denial. "Deny thyself," he said.

8.   The societal imagination is the idea of the opposite of good. The word opposite is the only foundation of imagination. Since Good is all, there can be no opposite of Good.

9.   This word of denial is strong and efficient to put away the sight of opposites. All your strange ideas of things in your life being opposite to what would please you best are instantly struck at their head or starting point. If you felt certain about this, the blow tells strongly there has never been but one man who seemed at all sure of his power through Truth. That was Jesus Christ. He felt ab-

solutely sure. Today we hear people say that if it were true they would feel sure too. That "if" is the protoplasm of matter which the mind of man is so continually putting out over the universe. Jesus never said "if;" he knew. Thus He wiped out everything He wished to have removed.

10. The world we look upon is the formulation of what would be if Spirit were not all. It is a beautiful imagination sometimes, and then again, it is terrible in its fury, and merciless in its action. We have imagined a regular succession of summer and winter, seed time and harvest. That idea we all based on the idea of another substance than Spirit. Shall the physical tell the Spirit of man what is true? It cannot tell us anything of God. "The earth is clean dissolve," said Isaiah [24:19]. But the creations of God are eternal. “For we know that if the earthly house of this tabernacle were dissolved, we have a building of God eternal in the heavens” [II Corinthians 5:1].

11. This eternal substance out of which the indestructible house is formed is Truth. Speaking Truth, we put away the stuff out of which material things are made and see the true house founded and built for us in Truth.

12. Speaking Truth is stepping along into our house. "Let us take with us words and go into our God." Now remember if we should not think anything at all, it should assume and perhaps sooner, give us a sight of our true eternal house.

13. The reason we are told to take with us words is because we incessantly insist upon thinking some definite thoughts. So the truer our thoughts are, the nearer in accord we shall be in

that which we wish to see. If thinking the way of
the world has put the wall of matter, hiding which
we wish to see, of course if we stop thinking badly
the veil must fall. This is silence. One can be silent
in thinking just as he can be silent in speaking. All
things are already finished. Our home is prepared.
Our happy conditions are fixed. We can see them
by refusing to see false notions.

14.   We may take down the veil of misery hung
up by our past ideas by denials of silence. The first
denial takes off a thick darkness, as it were, from
our own mind and feelings. The world in which we
seem to dwell looks quite miserable to us, even after we have become sound and well ourselves. Now
this world which looks so miserable is the outpic-
turing of our accusations against God.

15.   It is pictured by John the Revelator that
when the true angel speaks the four accusing angels will cease hurting the world. It is the seeming
hurt of our earth that we have imagined its inhabitants came forth from flesh by the action of its
laws. It is the simplest angel of accusing. When we
speak to hush the accusings we hear against our
neighbors, we agree with the angel who seals the
servants of the living God in their foreheads.

16.   We hasten the end of the material world by
hushing accusation. We may be sure to hush
within our own mind, which is where all accusings
start up, the very first one which is started against
every man and woman. Even the angels and archangels have not escaped our accusings. The gods
of the wonderful sculptors of Greek art were so full
of the stings of the first accusations that they are
no longer believed in at all. Zeus, Pallas Athena,
Venus, Bacchus, these were supposed to reign over

men. But men so accused them of the passions of earth that their names and their fame have departed. Phydias could not redeem them in the chaste marble. Only the angel of denial of their being so full of passions and appetites could touch them. All these gods primarily stood for some noble idea of the mind unmixed with evil or sin. This accusation is utterly withdrawn in Science and we do not hold any creature under the bondage of our thoughts after this, and forevermore.

17.   Moses took the springing forth of the earth from its chaos to the dominion of man upon it as a type or symbol of all mind rejecting ideas not true - imaginations not based on verity.

18.   To watch this process exactly as Moses described it would give even the materialist the key of his own studies. To follow Moses along is to understand Jesus Christ. To note the effect of the withdrawal of the accusation is to bring us to the name of the second false idea which we hold against the world. We have felt that the whole world is filled with liars. Our poetry tells us, "This world is all a fleeting show to man's delusions given." The Scriptures read, "these were all deceived, being in error."

19.   If we are deceived by anything or anybody, it is because we have been in error sufficiently to have deceived ourselves by accusing the world of deception. Paul, in I Corinthians 6:9, said, "Be not deceived." Moses said. "Even the night shall be light about us." Light is knowledge. To withdraw from the face of God the accusation that He is hidden from us, is to say: "I do not hold the world in deception."

20. Really the idea of things deceiving us and people deceiving us comes from the belief that God is invisible. It is our privilege to see God face to face. It is the knowledge of the nearness of God which comes when we hush the voice of the second angel of accusing by saying, "I do not hold the world in deception." There is no deception but a belief in deception.

21. If holding the idea that God is invisible has brought us to thinking that God is invisible in the faces and actions of our neighbors, in the dealings of times and circumstances, we will promptly proclaim that we do not believe in the invisibility of God and, therefore, do not hold the world in deception.

22. The child thinks that when he is grown to be a youth he will have what will please him better. The youth thinks that when he grows to be a man he shall have his fill. The man thinks time and industry or home and luck will favor him. But none of them are ever satisfied. This is the deception of human life. One thinks that gold will satisfy him, but he finds himself as restless on new lines as before he received it. Another thinks that if husband or brother or father would come home all would be well. But they hardly get safe on their feet when anxiety over things begins.

23. "Every heart knows its own bitterness" of waiting for its delight. This is the deceitfulness of riches. The whole deception is removed by proclaiming, "I do not believe in the invisibility of God, and do not hold the world in deception."

24. These two statements are the metaphysical meanings of Moses in the text, "Let there be Light." All the same there are other interrelations which

are perhaps more satisfactory to the student of Mind, the Spirit and the Intellect.

25.   The first statement of Light is,

"I do not believe in the invisibility of God."

The second is,

"I do not hold the world in deception."

Both of these are the setting free of the mind to see the world by drawing aside the curtains of darkness. The more obvious meaning of the passage is: The Spiritual intelligence of Mind is the true light symbolized by the sun. The intellect is the false light symbolized by the moon.

26.   Every Bible text can be pushed to a profound meaning. Even this has other meanings than the two just given.   For there is but One Light, One Sun, One Substance, One Being, Pure Manifest God. But while we are in any sense called upon to tell the whys and wherefores of this world which yields us material things, we will use the statement of metaphysicians from first to last. First, there is the seeming sun, moon and stars. We call the sun the true light of the world and the moon the false light. Then we say that God is visible, the world is in God's light. Then we know the I AM of man is God, so that he can truly say, "I am all." And the I AM is understood by itself as "I AM visible to Myself." Surely there is no injunction put upon us life seeking to know ourselves. And the injunction has intimated that we do not know ourselves. This is not true of the Spirit. And it is of the Spirit we must speak if we would have the Good visible.

27.   This is the true Light. John said, "The true Light now shineth." The light of the Spirit never ceases. It is here for us to realize every moment. Light is judgment. "There is a Spirit in man, and the inspiration of the Almighty giveth him understanding." This spirit is in man, and the inspiration of the Almighty does give him understanding. This spirit is shining as clearly in the thief as in Jesus Christ. If we speak of it as absent or hidden, we need to spend more time withdrawing our accusation of deception from the world in which we walk.

28.   It is our own fault if we do not see the light of God shining forth from the countenance and life of every living creature.

29.   It was taught by pantheism that "life slumbers in the stone, dreams in the plant, stirs in the animal, wakes in man." This was the attempt of the mind which has been taught the invisibility of God to see God in all things in spite of the books.

30.   Fichte, Shelling, Hegel and Cousin all saw that matter is mind. They studied mind as the former aspect of material things and got themselves more and more into darkness. What they needed was the light of these interpretations of Moses. For the instant we conceive as a supposition of intellect, that there is anything hiding God, we make it hidden. We must then drop the supposition and see clearly. The intellect, judging by what it has thrown forward upon the screen of human destiny, imagines God asleep, dreaming, awake. It imagines him as an invisible Being holding his children in hopes of happiness but giving them misery. These ideas are all the highest light of the nighttime of our destiny when the veil of imagination hides the sunshine of Truth.

31. God never sleeps, never dreams, never wakes. God is pure consciousness, pure light, pure understanding. God chooses to be the spirit of Jesus and the spirit of the prizefighter. Their appearance to us is our imagination of Spirit, Mind, Soul, Body. Even this appearance is the choice of God to test our judgment. God within us is to see God without us, and see God only. "I also choose their delusions, saith the Lord."

32. As a good teacher might give us some imaginary examples, so the law of Spirit, which is our schoolmaster, puts all this power of imagination within us and says, "Imagine what you please, choose what is true, report your conclusions." The God who says this never lets us get absolutely to the place where we are tempted by appearances above what we are able to resist. This God within us never lets us suffer and imagine beyond what we are able to hush any instant. This Light of God, perpetually shining, we may illuminate our world with at any moment.

33. "Ye are the Light of the world," said Jesus Christ. All the world in which we seem to dwell rests upon our notions. All the people with whom we associate wait upon our ideas. They cannot appear differently to us until we think differently of them. This is what Professor Huxley is trying to tell when he says that all matter is a mode of thought.

34. Professor Faraday published his opinion in the *Philosophical Magazine* in 1844 that physical objects must be immortal. This was his intellectual attempt to proclaim that as long as mind thinks certain ways all physical things must appear real.

35.   If the intellect imagines that there must be bacteria it will find bacteria. If, then, the intellect determines that these germs do not directly cause disease, there will have to be something between bacteria and disease. The whole matter rests upon the imagination of intellect.

36.   Sometimes the intellect gets to reasoning and observing with very accurate conclusions, but cannot make any connection between the conclusions and a better state of affairs. For instance, Hegel, the German philosopher (1770), said that the sensible world, or the world of physical sense, is an error, a delusion, void of Truth, that the being of these external things passes away like a stage show. He was right. Now if he had proceeded to say that if all these material things have their origin in delusion of our own mind, it is certainly our wiser plan to find out what is true and from a new kind of world, he would have struck the spiritual light at a glance.

37.   It is here at the edge of the precipice where their highest ideas of matter and thought can attain, that they stop.   The moonlight of intellect is unable to show the way farther. The colors and beauty of Truth at the end of intellectual heights no man can see save he of Spiritual Light. For, "the natural man receiveth not the things of the Spirit, for they are foolishness unto him, and he cannot know them, for they are spiritually discerned, but the spiritual man judgeth of all things and is himself judged of no man."

38.   What is the spiritual man's judgment of the world of matter? It is exactly like the intellectual man's highest judgment. What is that? Just what Hegel said: "It is void of Truth." "It is delusion."

But where the intellectual man is incompetent to tell how we shall have a true world, the spiritual man says, "Think Truth."

"So shall thy world grow polar to thee, slowly taught, and crystal out a new world like thy thoughts."

39. Every new thinker who comes along and studies the ideas of Kant, Fichte, Collier, Mill or Spencer, sees just as they see and stops, in wonder.

40. What a perfectly true message from his studies, Collier, the English metaphysician, gave us this in his great work, *Calvia Universalis* (1713), which means Inquiry after Truth of the Foundations of the Universe. Herein he explains that the external world is impossible. It is nonexistent. The whole world is within the circle of the mind.

41. What mind does he mean holds the world in its circle? He means the intellect which imagines objects by the million. Think what incessant pictures have been presented to us for ages which are only the speck of dust out of which Adam is made. Adam is error. The word means error. One word made the whole. The little word was "if."

42. If God, the Good, were not all, of course evil might be here. If God, the Spirit, were not all, of course material things must exist. If God were not the only Mind, other minds might be here. If the eternal Kingdom of Love and Goodness were not here, a temporal, hateful, deceitful world might surround us. But here at the point of admitting the unreality of the material world and the delusion of the mind which makes it, we proclaim that there is one world only—the world of God.

43. Here at the point where they all say that our will seems to will evil things into existence as well as good, we proclaim the lofty rock of Truth that there is but one will in us, which is the eternally good will of God. Here where the light of the intellect pales and dips below the morning horizon, where the unreality of the world, as it seems, is proclaimed, we take our stand in the light of the Truth, where the angel prophesied by John must stand and tell boldly our substance is Spirit, our thoughts are Truth, our world is God.

44. Here where the "I" of man is called the child of destiny, we proclaim every I AM to be Almighty God. There is no child save the thought of God. Where is not God his own Idea? God and His Idea are One. Is the idea of God made of matter or is it made of His own Substance? If God is One Presence, whose name is I AM, then I am that One Presence and my world is myself—Spirit, and not matter. I Am my own Light.

45. When I form my world there is none to oppose it. Which is better, since I form my world by my thoughts—that I should imagine a world peopled with dying, sick unhappy beings deluded by false hopes from birth to feeble age; or that I should assert, here at the central point where what I choose is what I shall experience, that I am King and Lord of Lords—willing goodness and beauty and happiness to myself and my world in which I live?

46. This is the choice the Central Judgment of me makes. I do not imagine what would be if Almighty Truth were not spoken. I Am Truth. I will not speak nor will I imagine foolishness.

47. This Light that shines forth from me is my free will. my will is not hampered or closed in upon me by folly. There is none to oppose me. None can come into my sphere save my own thoughts. And as maker of my world and its people, I know only peace. I have been God from the beginning: I am God now; I shall be God forever. Suppose that I have chosen to be Jesus Christ? Suppose that I have chosen to be Judas Iscariot? Suppose that I have chosen to have wars and pestilence and famine upon my sphere—out of what did the supposition arise? It arose out of nothing. Is nothing also the substance of which I am made, that I can make an imaginary world of horror? It is true that I am nothing and out of nothing I made the material universe. So I have permitted the word to go forth that I formed all things out of nothing. But I am all. I am the only Substance. Here on the topless heights of Truth I speak. "I am all, I am nothing." "I am nothing, I am all."

48. As matter I am nothing. As Spirit I am all. Out of nothing and from nothing I made matter. Imagination is nothing. I imagine. I imagine what I please. I know. Knowledge is all. Out of knowledge I speak my word into sight. But I imagine nothing. So my world is formed out of my knowledge.

49. These are the Lights of Moses. By day the sun of knowledge shines, and the evening time is as the morning with me for I imagine nothing. Therefore, I am the Light of the world. This is judgment at its best.

50. Moses knew this and proclaimed Me. Then he imagined death. But death is nothing, so Moses lives in My mind. To the world it is the privilege of

judgment to say, "I do not accuse you of deceitfulness."

51.   To that man or woman who claims sickness or pain it is good judgment to say, "I am not deceived by you. You are My own substance.   My substance is Truth. Therefore you are Truth. All is well with you."

52.   To Zeus, the God of Valor, I speak and take away the veil of accusing of unchaste thoughts. So Zeus, the God, shall be known as My thought of the valor of virtue. Now virtue is its own defense and safety without fighting to be safe; and thus Zeus shall return to Me. To Pallas Athena I proclaim that no veil of accusing hides the whiteness of the Hebrew *Shekinah*. So Pallas Athena shall come in the *Shekinah* to man.

53.   The substance of all things is My substance. The shadow of all things is My shadow. The symbol of all things is My symbol. Yet a symbol is nothing. Substance is all entirely.

54.   The universe is in Me. Yet the universe of matter is nowhere. All the universe of matter is contained within its mind, as My universe is contained within Me. This is the law of the seeming that it should always seem to be like Me. And thus the seeming claims to be My reflection. The shadow is opposite to its substance. So intellect with its world is opposite to Me.

55.   In the world of matter the intellect may search for Me during ages of looking, but I am not matter; and no intellect will be satisfied, but must be restless with seeing its world ever under its imagination as the moon sees the earth below it.

56. My intellect is God of its world as I am God over My world. Yet whenever the intellect proclaims "I am God," it shall be more restless and desolate than ever, for only "I Am God and there is none beside Me."

57. The intellect that says "I am God" shall never be definite as to what God should be and do in a world of matter. Therefore whenever intellect, which is the light of the flesh, shall speak My holy name, its strongest trait of thinking shall appropriate My power and dominion over the other thoughts of its realm and lo! it shall strengthen only in the trial that has before been its secret law of life. Its selfishness shall enlarge till all the earth where it walks can observe it. Its sympathy shall enlarge till it spoil it. The mortal shall not say, "I am God." Only Christ shall say "I am God."

58. The destruction that shall overtake them that shall call themselves by My name is by reason of every thought joining in My name, but the strongest shall have dominion.

59. The thought that is Jesus Christ shall come forth when the intellect keeps silence and man shall then have his eye single to know only My world within Me. My world is in the form of man. My likeness and express image is My idea. My one idea is Jesus Christ, not as intellect sees him, not as flesh conceives of him, but as the Spirit knows him.

60. Whoever is willing to lay down anxiety shall find Me. Whoever will lose his hold on material advancements shall find Me. He who persists in anxiety has never found Me. I am found in the light of the dropping of fears, the dropping of cares, the

dropping of efforts, the dropping of anguish, the dropping of subjugation to man or woman through fear or through desire to please.

61. I am One Light. I will not have a heart divided by thoughts bent on things of matter and hearts set on mechanical copies of My Kingdom of Peace. "If thine eye be single, thy whole body is Light." "The light of Me is the light of the body. Lo, I come."

62. In the volume of Daniel I tell My law of daily life to the heart of that man which is set upon the things of the earth. There I show how the light of the Intellect by its policies shall increase skill and perfect crafts. It shall hold the world in bondage by its gold with its ciphers or codes, which Daniel calls dark sayings, but My word in the mind of the tried and pure shall hurl this power down.

63. He then will persist in his early terrors, his fears, his anxieties; his clingings to matter shall still persist. My spirit of meekness shall find the night light as the day and the light of the moon shall no more be formed, but only the light of the knowledge of Me.

64. Read the whole book of Daniel. There you will find the last age of man under the light of symbol.

65. When there is a great knowledge of matter proclaimed and running to and fro in anxious excitement, there My Spirit is shining aloft and calling unto man to see light only in My light, to think only in Me. Then he shall not be deceived and he shall not accuse. He shall know how to speak to his world because I am his speech. "And there shall not be a lying tongue found upon the earth."

66. Whoever shall know this and still hold his own ways of thinking that evil is near him or threatens him, let him still keep his ways, but I am still shining, and when the will of the flesh yields its determination to rule in its own ways, I will light up that will with My fires. The will that is I AM is the Light of the world.

67. The will that determines to have things and laws whether I AM set that way or not, is the light of the world that is full of discord and strife. Its strife shall continue till My Will is all, till they give up the effort to bring things to pass, which I do not intend.

68. The loss of the false light is feigned by the judgment that lets now My Will be done over its will, and through its will, and in its will.

The strength to do all things upon the earth is ours. To see Jesus Christ fact to face is to be Jesus Christ. To be Jesus Christ is to die to all sin. To die on the Cross is to yield all our thoughts to the words, "I am nothing." To rise from the Cross is to come forth with the words, "I am all." To yield on the Cross the full growth of our imagination is to say, "Of mine own self I can do nothing." To raise into the third strength from this rejection to all our works of the mind is to speak forth boldly: "I can do all things." "All power is given unto me."

"For whosoever will save his life shall lose it: but whosoever will lose his life for my sake, the same shall save it" [Luke 9:24].

LESSON NINE

Face to Face

1.   John the Revelator speaks of four beasts in the midst of the throne and round about the throne of God.

2.   These beasts are the four strengths within our mind. Of all living things the beasts of the field are the strongest. No man is as strong as an ox in that state of strength unchanged by the spirit which the men of the world exhibit. But the beasts of all countries are strong. Therefore, in the Book of Revelation, always translate the word "beast" as strength of mind, and you will almost have a key to every other expression that John the Revelator used. Indeed, one figure translated exactly right is enough for a spiritually-minded reader to interpret all other passages by.

3.   Animals are the strongest symbols of the strong ideas people have held which they never applied to themselves. One can project his thoughts into space and have a strong beast at some great distance rear its fierce head among the jungles.   This is the way the beasts of the forest are formulated. All the same, they are only symbols

of strength. They have a real substance in the spirit of man thinking a noble idea. If one thinks the strong idea within himself, assimilates it within his own mind, he will be as strong as the beast himself. He will appropriate the strength to himself and no wild beast or strong domestic animal will be seen as the representation of his idea. All outward things represent what we have not assimilated. The farther off our ideas seem to us, the farther off their representatives will be. The civilized man is the one who has the idea that, if he feels strongly angry, he ought not to strike or slay his neighbor. This idea of "ought not" pushes the feeling of anger far into the hidden jungles of his mind. It is a strong feeling but it has power. The savage man feels the anger and strikes. Therefore, he lives near the lion, the panther, the tiger. The "ought not", which the civilized man teaches himself, finally puts the beasts of the forest out of the forest.

4. The teachings of "ought not" come over the face of the mind and the mind is subdued. Then all the fierce and savage things are gone. But though they are gone they are not gone. They as savage beasts are symbols. Only the symbol can disappear; the substance remains. The true beast is the spiritual strength which in Revelation, fourth chapter, John sees.

5. The first one, John says, is a lion. He is referring wholly to the spiritual quality. There is one spiritual quality mind has, which it has wrapped round with a forest. The spiritual quality which makes mind strong as a lion is the strength to endure. Strength to endure is not strength to bear

afflictions. It might be called strength to ignore. Now, the true name of this strength is purity.

6. "To the pure, all things are pure." The name of purity is chastity. To the chaste in heart nobody is adulterous, no one is greedy, no one seems to be full of wrong motives. "The Knight's Tale" of Chaucer has the hint of how safely a mind may walk in a forest of wild animals, if it knows nothing of the claims of appetites for unclean things. The White Cross legions have for one of their mottoes, "My strength is as the strength of ten because My heart is pure."

7. The lion of the tribe of Judah was Jesus Christ the sinless. But what strength is there equal to the strength of the leviathan, the whale of the seas of ancient times? No land animal of today can equal it. Job says: "Canst thou draw out the leviathan with an hook? None is so fierce that dare stir him up," [Job 41:10]. Then he compares himself with the leviathan which cannot be caught or mastered. "Who then is able to stand before Me?" he asks. This is because he has exposed the strength of his word. He uses the terrible and unconquerable leviathan which even the strong rifle balls of the guns of modern warfare cannot kill as a symbol of the strength of his words which he has uncovered. He is not prophesying of a time when there shall be none of these sea monsters, but yet the whole Book of Job is a fitting accompaniment to the Book of Revelation which tells us that "there shall be no more sea," when the right doctrine shall be preached.

8. The word of truth spoken vehemently in the midst of the world of seeming opposites is put forth in the Book of Job. The mind strong in the fulfill-

135

ment of the words it has spoken is put before us in Revelation.

9.   The strength of the leviathan gave way to the terrible strength of the behemoth of the land. And then the strength of the coarse, brute force of the behemoth gave way to the sagacious strength of the lion which is king of beasts of sagacity, boldness, endurance.   The lion is the last terrible animal the earth of matter shall ever know.   When he passes off the earth, the strength that remaineth shall be the strength of the rest to the people of God. The strength of rest to the people of God shall be first shown forth by their ability to endure, to hold on to their faith through seemings of evil, actually making them nothing by ignoring them.

10.   The strength of ignoring is the strength of denial. The strength of denial is not in the denial, but in what is exposed by denial. The strength of the light is not in the curtain which we pull aside to let the light in, but in the light which is exposed by the withdrawal of the curtain. So the withdrawal of the veil of matter by denial exposes the spiritual strengths which are the inheritance of the sons of God.

11.   The science of Christ teaches the withdrawal of the accusation of the world against all life that it has the choice of reproduction of its kind. The hunger of the self-increasing is only a symbol of the self-increasing power of an idea. Every idea can feed on other ideas until it has eaten them up and must make other ideas. This eating power of an idea is also a symbol, for in truth there is no self-increasing power but Jehovah *Jireh.*

12.   The first strength which the mind exhibits in relation to the world in which it has folded itself by taking down the accusing curtain of belief which there is in the mind that shows living things and appetite or desire for anything whatsoever, is the strength to ignore. There is no desire. There is no hunger. There is no appetite. There is no hope. There is no aspiration. There is no ambition. There is no avarice. There is no crying. There is no claiming. There is no seeking. There is no reaching out after anything. These denials are all included under the withdrawing of our accusation which the mind makes against living creatures.

13.   All life is God. There is no life except God. So all accusation is against God. To give forth an accusation is to hide with a veil of flesh the marvelous strength of the spirit.

14.   The Science of Christ teaches us the manner of withdrawal of accusation both by declaring with the boldness of Job, 'There is no lustful passion and sensual appetite." and also by proclaiming to the living things of all creation, "I withdraw my accusations." This is as if one drew a curtain to the right and to the left. The strength of Purity springs forth.   The power of Defense, which is chastity itself, rouses like a lion from its lair.

15.   Moses spoke of letting the waters bring forth living creatures. The waters are our words. Words may be silently held within our mind or may break forth as speech. The words of the mind are called the affections of the mind by Swedenborg. These affections of the mind are called the creatures of the sea. Affections are the things we choose.   We may choose to think of things we do not love, as man may choose to think a man has an appetite

for sense indulgence. But this is not true. It is an affection to think what we do not love to think. It is a creature that stays with us. It belongs to our mind's idea.

To refuse the idea is to be free from it. Job refused almost every idea that was presented to him. This gave him the strength of creation. He commanded that day to perish wherein he was born of flesh. He would only admit that he was born of God. He refused to be deceived. He would not know any doctrine but the ideas of spirit. He thus took off from the face of spirit the accusation of deception. Thus he saw clearly how a man's fears make gruesome shades which show forth as failure of goods. His own goods had failed by being deceived. He saw how his own health had failed by being deceived into accusing the Spirit of sending disease. He saw how death and destruction had seized his family by reason of his accusation against God of sending all the hardships of life.

16. Then he arose and withdrew the accusation. He denied the appearance. This gave him the strength of the Calf of Revelation, which is the strength of daring. He dared face all his friends in council. To him their arguments were nothing at all. His boldness and daring were the boldness and daring of youth. No man's experience went before him to guide him in meeting his companions with arguments to prove that he was strong as the leviathan of the sea and the behemoth of the land.

17. He sees himself strong under the tree of Omnipotence as the young behemoth. To any mind that is able to refuse to believe lies when he hears them, the strength of the calf of behemoth is given. This is the strength and beauty of youth. It

is the first sign of yielding to lies whether against your friends or neighbors in acceptance of them, when age begins to show its wrinkles and toughens and darkens the skin.

18. Look at the thickening and fast-aging countenance of those who accuse the world of being a dark, deceitful abode of liars and cheats and injustice. They darken and wrinkle at the first experience of thinking that cheating is a part of the way the world gets its successes. The callow youth of a man refuses to think that evil can get the better of good. The refusal to think of unchastity uncovers great strength. In the callow youth of a man he feels the promise of a future of glory by the ways of honor and virtue. Temptations fling themselves around him and good people are pictured as bad by those in whom he believes. He hears the voice of some mind in whose fealty and truth he believes telling of the wrong actions of some innocent person. He believes the deception. His first wrinkle sets into his darkened face. He thus hides the strength of the beauty of youth.

19. The young woman is told of the evils of the world into which she has come. Her husband's character is supposed by her neighbors to be part of the hidden iniquity of mankind. Those neighbors set the first darkness upon the face of beauty and youth. Its early wrinkles begin. Her faith in the victory of virtue over vice is met by the appearance of the triumph of vice over virtue. She believes suddenly in the power of evil. This is the darkening and wrinkling time just opened.

Why should she not be the young and beautiful beast of the rejection of all deception? Job refused to be deceived into thinking that in a world created by the Good, owned by the Good, occupied by the Good, evil could have any power or place. Whoever refuses to believe in evil report, refuses the shadow of old age. John, the Revelator, calls it the calf of behemoth. The young strength of the spirit, with all the world reporting evil, yet stands up and proclaims:

I refuse to be deceived by evil report.

I refuse to believe the words of my neighbor against the living creatures. I do not think they hide iniquity under the cloak of good manners. I do not think they get rich by cheating. I do not accuse the worst appearing man or woman of being a liar, a cheat, a deceiver. I do not see anything but good in the presence of God. Though you tell me of hardships and sorrows I will not believe you. I love and trust you, but I cannot be deceived into believing that you are in earnest when you tell me things that are evil concerning the life of man and of beast. The lion is as innocent and harmless as the lamb. I will not be deceived into thinking that he hides hate and ferocity under his strong face. I know that his life is God, the Good. I know that his mind is God, the Good.

20.   I am not afraid. I trust you utterly as the presence of God, but I will not hear you call any man or woman or child a treacherous neighbor or a deceitful character. Nothing against My family will I believe though it all might seem blackly true. I do not heed what is told Me of the deception of people or the seeming failure of the upright man or woman to hold their own in the world. Nothing can deceive Me. I do not accuse, neither do I agree with the accusations of the world as deceiving us

with fair promises and giving us apples of Sodom with disappointment.

God is the only Presence, the only power, the only action. In God is My knowledge. This is My choice. This is My affection of My conscious mind. I bring it forth to show the earth a sweet thought. Wherever My thoughts run, there the waters of earth shall be filled with sweet and refreshing life.

21. The knowledge of God shall cover the earth as the waters fill the sea. This is My flowing, clear, conscious mind. In it is the sunshine of light. On My mental sphere I will have the water ever telling that the sun shines. Truth is bright. Spirit rules. Goodness comes off triumphant. It makes no difference what seems to be true.

22. I proclaim that the mind of man is the mind that is God. The life of man is the life that is God. Nothing can deceive me and I do not think it is trying to deceive Me. I am the Truth of God and I see the Truth of God. Hereby the veil of the temple is rent in twain and God is justified of me.

23. Thus one triumphs over the laws of the flesh. This is the fixing into the face and the gleaming forth of the eye of the young, the behemoth. This is the law of youth and beauty, the external youth and beauty of truth, which cannot be deceived and thinketh no deception of anybody. Whoever believes in mesmerism accuses the world of deceptive strength. So shall he have the reputation of being old and well stricken in years. He shall lack the strength of youth. Whoever believes in psychological power accuses the race of deception and his face is darkened and wrinkled with age. He shall not show forth the strength of youth.

Whoever believes in hypnotism as a spiritual power or as having a law believes in the way of deception. He agrees with lies. He cannot show forth the second strength or the youthful sign of eternal freedom.

Whoever accuses any man or woman of being able to hold another in bondage is deceived by an appearance, for there is no bondage and no power of bondage. All is spirit. All is freedom of spirit. Age is the reputation of all who are under bondage or are thinking of bondage. Age is only a claim and it only belongs to those who have first accused the world of some sense appetites, and second, of being deceitful through holding powers unlike the Divine Jehovah, Jesus Christ.

24. At this point the sages let go their hold on youth. The difficulty of keeping the truth in the midst of opposition caused them to mourn over the power of evil. Hair turned gray and eyes grew dim at the idea of the failure of goodness and truth to win their way. The boldness of callow youth and the courage of young faith stop. The calf beast of Revelation steps not forward. This is called the effort to renew and reform the world in which we walk—the second treatment of man—the second step nearer seeing the world as God sees it.

25. Looking back to your first lessons in the Science of Truth, do you remember how you called those men and women sick and disordered whom your own beliefs in evil had held in bondage of unwholesome thoughts of deception? You learned the cleansing power of denial to each of them by whatever words the Spirit gave you utterance, to teach that their health and strength may be uncovered in your sight. The meeting of many such people has

given you quick cleansing powers. Today you do not meet sickness. It is put far away as the beasts of the jungles are hunted down in the African forests. You hear of sickness but you do not meet it. You hear of the restlessness and dissatisfaction of mankind. You hear of their jealousy and revenge.

Why do you hear in that far away place of your mind that the stagnation of hope in the minds of the masses may be your lot by and by? Why do you feel that the denials of Science have not wrought all their mission? It is because you have come into a state of believing that the words of Science are rich and good in putting aside bodily ailments, and small events of sickness, but your hope swells not into the free untrammeled strength of man. The third strength is not exposed in you to handle your world.

26. The third beast was the strength of the face of man. The face of man as he truly is has never been seen because there has been thrown over the world the accusation of sin. The full glory of the Son of God was not exposed even to the disciples of Jesus, because of the accusations of the world that were between Him and them. Whoever should remove from his mind the idea of mankind being selfish, envious, jealous, malicious, revengeful and cruel would take from his face the curtain of sin. The face of the Son of God looks straight into your face from the countenance of the criminal and the beggar. Whoever removes from his mind the thought that these are sinful and wretched must first take from his mind the idea that there is sin in the presence of God.

27. It is well to know that in the closet of home is the place from whence your thoughts go into the

world to preach the gospel, heal the sick, cast out demons, raise the dead. It is there that doing it unto the least of the world exactly as unto the greatest, the cleansing from sin, is wrought. It is in the closet that we speak what ought not to be and preach boldly what ought to be. This is the preparation for the world which, being made makes the day easy and possible.

28. There is no sin; it is all unreality. It is but the imagination of mind risen from its state of being deceived with respect to the presence of God on into the idea of defense from its neighbors. This is the progress of the void or vague feeling of what might be if God were not all. That feeling in the mind of man even without words starts the possibility of future evils. The imagination of another presence besides the Divine kindness of God is a definite deception.

29. Some minds imagine a definite action. They take the formless fear that lies like a molten sea within them and stir it into one thought of the evil that might come to a child or a friend or themselves. The fear thus definitely told starts the vipers and snakes in the grasses. If it is kept going by agreement with other believers in evil or the coming of hurts, these creatures appear in the fields where they walk and look out from the faces of mankind.

30. Hold on to your imagination of what might be if God were not all, and everything pertaining to your lot in life will show the viper. You can understand Job, who said that "the thing I feared has come upon Me." Everything about us looks into our faces with our fears and hopes and our faiths all marked in strong lines. If we have felt every event

full of bitterness or pain for us, we have been vaguely afraid of coming to want.

31. Maybe we have thought of what it would be if we should have to give up some possession. We thought of this possibility till it became plain to us how it would seem to be without it. Then we went away and forgot our fear in the busy works of our art. But the germ that is warmed by the imagination and the fear of the mind keeps on growing. The forgetfulness of mind keeps on growing. The forgetfulness of mind is no safety from its past thoughts. Only forgiveness by the blood of Jesus Christ can annul these imaginations, which the mind has no right to imagine while the infinite sea of the thoughts of God lay in full sight.

32. Why should we choose to imagine evil while the good is true? Why should we think of what would be hard to bear if it should overtake us when it is not true that it is here or ever could overtake us except in pure imagination?

33. Mind is all. It stirs into definite forms its ideas and turns them into arable soil of the universe as fishes spawn and forget. But as the fishes live and come into sight of those who have spawned them, so our thoughts we have chosen to think come speaking through the beggars, the convicts, the failures, the hardships, the want of our lot.

34. Forgiveness of sin is needed when our first imaginations have grown and fruited into men with hatred and venom or into shedding of blood. What is the shedding of blood? If blood is life then we must shed our life for them. We must die. And what is death that we must take it upon ourselves?

As it is written: "He that would save his life must lose it and he that would lose his life for My sake shall find it."

35.   In the first place it is surely explained that all our efforts are made to bring our good that belongs to us unto us. Every thought we think is with the effort to bring our own good into our lot. When our imaginations of evil have reached the actions of selfish cruelty, it is our first thought to get utterly rid of them. To think utter destruction is to think of death. So death, which we imagine is good for us, begins to gnaw at the vitals of our bodies and all our environments. At first birth of anger or grief against thoughts or actions of mankind, death starts its ruthless gnawing. Thus death is the end of sin. It is the end of the belief in sin. Is death then the highest demonstration of good when an imagination has run a vague fear into a definite thought which has grown, till like all imagination it has become selfish, envious, jealous, malicious, revengeful, cruel?

36.   Yes, death is the highest demonstration of Good for sin. Death is the remission of sin. The sinner shall plead for the washing of his sins away. He shall plead for forgiveness. Do we mean that there should be death of the body, death of life? No, we mean death of the imagination—the wiping of it out of our mind from its first vague fear to its appearance in the faces and actions of men. Jesus Christ, the companion of thieves and publicans, must be hidden, that Jesus Christ, the companion of God, only may abide in us. All the nature of us which is capable of seeing good may be left. Jesus Christ is no longer the companion of thieves. He is companion of the soul, of the thief by his laying

down his whole nature which is capable of seeing the Divine of mankind.

37. He hung on the cross of denial and affirmation to the utmost death of all imagination that in truth he might see all his world and companion and strengthen all souls. Today the redeemed Jesus Christ is companion of your soul and my soul. In us He sees no sin. To Him only our soul in its glory of goodness is visible. "Who shall save us from our sins save he that seeth no sin in us." And thus, companion of our soul, He strengthens us in our death. His death is ours. By His death we see our imagination with those shadows we have wrapped around ourselves drop away. This is the end of sin, when we know the meaning of His death.

39. Did he then indeed die? Did the Christ suffer death for our sins? The Christ took our sins of the race and folded them around as a mantle that they might be slain. But the Christ was untouched.

40. To see this Truth, to believe this way, is to see imagination folded within the crucifixion with Jesus on Calvary's mountain. To see this in truth and what it means is to feel the imagination of evil fall away. To see the Christ alive and still near is to be risen with Him in glory.

41. Here, risen with the Christ, who gives glory for pain, we know our oneness with Christ. Our soul is united in peace and love. We forget our former imaginations. They are erased by our knowledge of truth. The shackles of sin have fallen from us. No man can work the work of vengeance or hatred upon us. No event can transpire with pain or failure for us. Jesus Christ is sufficient for

us. Here at this death of the whole of our past the rising of the strength of the man Jesus Christ is given unto us. The man of action who can do miracles by the word of his speaking is in us. "I in them, Thou in Me."

42. The strength to do all things upon the earth is ours. To see Jesus Christ face-to-face is to be Jesus Christ. To be Jesus Christ is to die to all sin. To die on the cross is to yield all our thoughts to the words "I am nothing." To rise from the cross is to come forth with the words "I am all." To yield on the cross the full growth of our imagination is to say, "Of mine own self I can do nothing." To rise into the third strength from this rejection to all our works of the mind is to speak boldly: "I can do all things. All power is given unto Me."

43. To read the sign of our thoughts in the things of the world is to know what we have thought. To reject all the past according to the teachings of Jesus Christ is to go by his example. Our mind drops its past and its present ideas whatever they may be. It looks to the Christ of Itself. This is its cross.

44. From the cross we go forth the companion of soul. Hid with Christ, the Simeons of sorrow may sweep over the globe, but we know them not. The armies of anger may rush past the nations, but to us they are absent. Imagination of evil from the vague fear of indefiniteness to the grown pain of cruelty may be gone from him who lets drop from the mind the agreements with fear or evil.

45. All is Mind. That which I see of Jesus on the cross is within my own mind. I am with Jesus Christ now risen from the laying down of even my denials and affirmations. The time is past when

the soul needs to speak of what is within the sight of material things with laws and men, with crudities and sin. These have been left in the tomb. Even the cross has tumbled to dust in my mind. Thereby I know that even my denials and affirmations are ended. I am risen with Christ into a kingdom where the memory that there were thoughts to be denied and living words to be spoken is dropped.

46. The face of the man Jesus Christ is forever with Me. Great works are easy, and masterful deeds are simple for Me. Yet it is not I, but Christ with Me that doeth the works. If there is ill spoken of Me, I do not know it. I only know there is no ill. I see forever the face of the risen Christ in all faces of men.

47. All nature is filled with Christ. The substance that holds them together is Christ. The "I AM" of the stone is Christ. The "I AM" of me is Christ. There is nobody to tell me of sin, for there is only Christ. There is nobody to hurt me, for there is only Christ. There is no sickness, for there is no sin to make sickness. There is only Christ. There is no death, for death is swallowed up in victory. Death was the letting fall of imaginations. These are all let fall.

48. Christ is All. Thus death and hell are ended.

49. The imaginations which ran their full length into the idea of sin among men and pain in our lot are led captive by Truth. In all our world there is only Christ. This is the meditation of the closet whose strength of doing shall be proclaimed on the housetops. That which is true in My mind as I sit alone facing Christ is that which I shall meet in My

intercourse with the world. Here let us have our feet shod with the preparation of the Gospel.

The "I" that fills all the universe is Jesus Christ.

50.   The "I" that has cleansed and redeemed the world is Jesus Christ.

51.   Jesus Christ in me is Omnipotent God.

Omnipresent Omnipotent Omniscient

The very fact that nations of the earth wrangle over the character of a personal God show that there is no God like their descriptions. When the people find out the laws of numbers, they never dispute each other as to whether five and five make ten. The Arabian, the Roman, the Englishman, the South Sea Islander, will be figuring on the same principle; and when they meet in the class room, they will know the principles are correct. Principle stands at the center of Life

"*...a house divided against itself cannot stand.*" [Matthew 12:25]

LESSON TEN

The Operation of Principle

1.   Seneca, the Stoic, was once writing about keeping the mind poised and sane so that the environments would be orderly.   He wished mankind to snatch themselves from the universal bondage of fear. To do this would be the salvation of the whole world.

2.   He said: "Sanity lies in self content and self trust. The blessed life is that which needs not addition from without. To be wishful—to be dependent on benefits— is to be unfinished. You have only to will to be good. The soul will then feed itself and grow of itself and exercise itself.   You should will to be free—to snatch yourself from this universal bondage of fear, which is the oppression of mankind, you must free yourself from the fear of death and then of poverty."

3.   To begin in childhood with agreeing with one ugly proposition concerning human life, will end in some defect of body and misfortune in environment.   Doctor the Mind with right thoughts and the cure is sure.

4.   Socrates said that men act wrongly only because they have wrong judgments.

5.   It is easy for some to reduce all outward appearance to a mental cause. They will apply the mental cure and the appearance is gone. To others the physical cause is most reasonable and they seek for that. They even chase down the wrinkles and flatulency of age to the microbes that cause them, and apply the acids that have power to kill the microbes.

6.   There is hardly any curing outward conditions by handling their physical, visible causes. Causation is mental. "The ultimate cause of all things is invisible," it is said. Hence there is no study so infinitely worthwhile as the study of causation. The cause of all that is, is mind. Therefore to get truly wise one should study mind. Mind is God. Thus to get truly wise one should study God.

7.   In studying causation and finding it is Mind— and studying Mind and finding it is God— do we then find the cause of disease to be God, since God is cause? No, we find there is no cause for disease. This is the result of studying Mind. We find that there is but one Mind thinking thoughts. That mind is thinking only beauty, holiness, wisdom.

8.   In the Infinite Sea of that Mind, diseases and thoughts of diseases take up no more room than shadows in a lake of clear water. This is the peculiar effect of the study of Mind, *vis:* that only the Mind of God has any reality in it to the student of Mind.

9.   To the student of bones there is nothing worthwhile but bones. Does he grow strong and

vigorous in his bones by fastening all his thoughts on bones? Judging from the appearance of such students, we must conclude that the study of bones is unhealthy.

10. But many imagine that such study of bones results in the skillful handling of deranged and broken bones and therefore is a benefit to mankind. But if Mind is the cause of all things, do you not see that to be getting ready for broken and disarranged bones would be the hurrying of people to breaking and disarranging bones as fast as ever they could in order to bring into visibility the thoughts of those students? Who shall make a broken bone save he who thinketh faithfully upon broken bones? This is on the same principle exactly as "Who shall save us from our sins, save He who seeth no sin in us?"

11. Who is the true line of saving from broken bones, save he that seeth in God's universe no brokenness? This is the whole law of saving out of appearances reduced to one sentence. What we look for we find. What we think, we see. But there will not be any true seeing, except we look for what is truly made already.

12. There are four strengths to which our world in which we walk will vibrate, if by reason of our ideas with relation to our world, we have brought them forth. These four strengths are: the strength to endure—the strength to dare—the strength to do—the strength to be silent.

13. The strength to be silent implies the strength to speak, for silence gives wisdom. The hush of the voice is the noblest speech.

14.   Jesus Christ set the example of silence under calumny, under accusation, under persecu-
tion.   There are two words which the strength of
silence teaches; and there is a standpoint from
which the Mind always speaks, when it is pro-
foundly silent.   It always speaks from the standpoint of the Spirit and lets that Spirit speak its own
holy name, through the silence. Then the teaching
of the one always has been, when he opens his
lips, that there is no Substance, no Life, no Intelligence, no name except "I am Substance, I am Life,
I am Intelligence, I am God." He does not hesitate
to proclaim that God is his only name. If there is
any reasoning from that standpoint of Spirit you
will see that from that standpoint your Substance
is God. Your name is God.

15.   It is promised to those who shall speak
from the spiritual standpoint— "I will put My name
upon them." It is the day of the baptism of Omnipotence when the I AM of Jehovah is spoken
through you.

16.   But there is a denial that balances that affirmation. It is "I am nothing." The intellect and
the senses must be willing to be nothing. The
tastes of the senses must be forgotten. The decrees
of the intellect must fall into nothingness. The
standpoint of evil and matter is no standpoint at
all. As the Mind has been speaking long and much
from that standpoint, it naturally mixes its mental
and its audible proclamations of Godhead with the
intellectual and physical remembrances it has
held, through early experiences. Therefore when
one is speaking from the spiritual name "I am
God," he must follow it by the proclamation of intellect "I am nothing." At the poise between these

two statements is your power of demonstration. At the gateway between "I am God," and "I am nothing" stands Jesus Christ. Jesus Christ is mediator between God, as he is and man as he seems. With Jesus Christ the whole world is God and the whole world is nothing. With Jesus Christ "All is God" and "There is no God." He sees the God of this world is Satan, who is a liar from the beginning and the father of all lies. Thus, as lies are nothing and Satan is all lie, he is reigning over anybody or any power reigning over you. If you believed in Satan, you have had Satan reigning over you and have been describing Satan when you have described your God.

17. You have preserved the character of God by the words, Life, Truth, Love, Spirit, Intelligence, Omnipresence, Omnipotence, Omniscience. But in every description you have made heretofore, you have been describing a Satan. For God reigns over none. God is all. God is the there and the here. To say God is here is to feel that God is in you. To say that God is there is to walk toward God gladly.

18. But to say that God is not in this or in that, is to tell of a Satan showing partiality. God is not a partial God. To speak of God as loving us one day and displeased with us another is to speak of a Satan, for God, the I AM, is unchangeable Love. To speak of God as being more taught by one religion than another is to speak of Satan, for God is the Substance of all religions.

19. So the proclamation 'There is no God" puts Satan, the God of the world, away forever. It leaves the heart poised in the hand of Divine Goodness. Here is the ability to demonstrate. Here is Jesus Christ.

At the gateway between the God that is true and the God that is Satan stands Jesus Christ, the Mediator. Whoever says "All is God" and "There is no God, touches the meaning of the name Jesus Christ. For between the world with its policies that make life so hard for mankind, and the Spirit, with its love, making life so easy, is Jesus Christ understanding them both.

To Jesus Christ death is nothing. Life is easy. To Jesus Christ all power was given. To Jesus Christ pain is nothing. Peace is his substance. The riches of God are all his. Yet of his human nature he knew he could do nothing. Thus he understood humanity and God. This was his healing power.

As the Mind cannot get the power to do anything except by having faith in itself, as it is written by Seneca, so the management of this world in which we walk is not possible save by being equally poised between the world of Spirit and the no world of matter. It is equally important that we tell what we do not believe as what we do believe. It is as important to be Omnipotent God as to be meek and lowly of heart.

It is not possible to reach the fourth strength, which is the strength of silence, and the strength of wisdom, till we are Jesus Christ in the poised place between God and Satan—the God who is truly God and the Satan who seems to be God. This is silence. With this knowledge the thousand years of Satan let loose are ended. For it is in Truth that Jesus Christ binds him who is God of this world and casts him down with all who serve him. It is only possible to get poised between Spirit and matter knowing matter as nothing and handling it easy, and charged full with Spirit, knowing it as

Omnipotence, if the mediatorial office of Jesus Christ be given the place of our Mind.

20.   The God of this world is Satan, who sometimes claims to be honorable name and sometimes claims to be riches.

21.   But there is Spirit riding high in the heavens. Jesus Christ with his feet on the riches of the sea and master of them through knowledge of God, to Him the riches of the earth are nothing, to Him the God of the world is nothing. To Him Spirit is all. To be Jesus Christ is the poise between the strength to do all things and the silence of infinite wisdom.

22.   To look out over the world as we see it and from the closet of meditation to declare "I do not believe in Satan, I believe in Jesus Christ/' is to be set free from the God of the world and poised in the presence of Christ. It is the binding forever of the powers of evil. To look out over the world and proclaim from the closet of meditation "I do not believe in evil, I believe only in God" is to feel the clutch of evil losing its hold.

23.   There is a power in the poise (between) the definite statement of what we do not believe and what we do believe which is safety from the sight of violence or misery.

24.   Looking back upon your lesson on chemicalization, you will see mention made of violence through the conflict of evil against God. This is the conflict of evil against God. This is the conflict you have in your world through not having your feet shod with the preparation of the closet, which is meditation.

25.   The world will show no chemicalization to you if you speak boldly "I do not believe in the God of this world — I believe in Jesus Christ.

26.   The very fact that the nations of the earth wrangle over the character of a personal God shows that there is no God like their descriptions. When the people find out the laws of numbers, they never dispute each other as to whether five and five make ten.   The Arabian, the Roman, the Englishman, the South Sea Islander, will be figuring on the same principle; and when they meet together in the class room, they will know the principles are correct if the answers are correct.

27.   They will quickly detect a blunder. They will see at once if their teacher is wiser than a memorizer of rules by his demonstrations.   There will not be one dissenter to the idea that five and five make ten, on the measurements of solids and the computations of distances.

28.   God is Principle. There is no personality to the God of Truth any more than there is a personality in numbers. Whoever loves the science of numbers and practices their combinations will get on into understanding of numbers. He will be able at his calculations. His face will begin to look polished and refined. He is studying Principle. Principle is polished and refined. He is studying Principle. Principle is polished like a sea of crystal. Principle is fine and clear.

29.   There is no limit to the refinement of the law of the mathematician who proceeds in his study and holds fast to his love of mathematics.   The Principle he is dealing with is God—accurate, reliable, unchangeable Truth. The Jealous God of Moses— True. Jealousy is the integrity of principle.

160

True Principle attended to, marks the face and form with its accuracy. True Principle neglected, is just as accurate in marking the face with signs of neglect.

30.   The mathematician who loves his Principle better than anything else will grow beautiful, refined, upright. The mathematician who neglects mathematics for the banquet hall, the racecourse, the gambling table, dividing his love of mathematics with his love of some pleasures, will show the broken lines and patches of a divided affection.

31.   "A house divided against itself cannot stand."

32.   Principle stands at the center of the circle of life.

33.   Whichever way we proceed to think, its law of cause and effect is visible.

34.   The man who loves the banquet hallmarks his face with his hall. It is Principle that one is marked with his love.

35.   The beauty of Principle is that a man may choose to love the action of Principle by and through whatever lines of its law he pleases. He may choose the art of gambling and pursue it to the extent of finding that there is no chance. What seems like chance to the ordinary observer is but the operation of a fixed law. The motion of the arm determines which way the dice shall drop. Therefore whoever understands the motions of arm can better calculate upon the spots on the dice. It is his Science.

36.   If a man keeps on figuring and calculating up such operations as throwing of dice his face will

look studious and refined because he is studying Principle. Now if he divides his time and attention between computing about elbows and angles of distance and the slaughterhouse, his face will show the broken lines and patches of a divided attention.

37.   The study of Principle must be the study of One. Now this One is God.

38.   The study of One Principle through the phenomena of dice boxes is slow and tedious. The study of One Principle through the Arabic numeral is slow and tedious. The study of One Principle through the phenomena of matter is slow and tedious.

39.   Thousands upon thousands of years have not brought mankind to where the knowledge of incidence and reflection, of contraction and recontraction, have brought the satisfactory state which the heart is set upon finding.

40.   The sun has been worshipped through the phenomena of his courses, but the One Principle is not yet come upon by his worshippers. The stars have been worshipped as God, but their devotees are not nearer the One Principle in understanding than were the sun worshippers.

41.   The animals have all been tried. Images of grotesque imaginations have been set up. But all who have called them God, have been as far from being like what the divine instinct at the centre of mind is satisfied with as the mathematician, the gambler, the banqueter.

42.   They have all said that they see how the Principle is operating toward greater nearness to themselves, but they do not feel at one with it in

the satisfaction of being it, which every heart is seeking to be.

43. Thus the great question for mankind to consider is surely not "What shall I study?" but "what shall I not study?"

44. This question silences or stops his efforts. It silences or stops his thinking. He then knows what is meant by the inspired injunction of the psalmist "Be still and know that I am God."

45. Whatever any mind stops doing he starts over again. He strikes one. Here is the true God— the One at the center. The least movement of mind now determines what the outward actions shall be and what the reasoning must be.

46. Here at the poised center one finds that it is his choice, which he shall demonstrate, his God Head or his personality, his principle or his passions.

47. He may say, "I am King of Kings, and Lord of Lords," or he may say, "I am a little child with no intelligence and no rights." He may be Jesus Christ or he may be Guillaume. He may be master or serf at his word. He may be companioned by kings and princes of power, wisdom, riches, or companioned by beggars, unlettered, ignoble. It is entirely a matter of choice. The word of choice sets a train of actions into sight which nothing can interfere with till the same mind suddenly or gradually stops thinking along that line and begins at his center. Demonstration is visibility. Visibility is manifestation. Principle is not manifest as itself till satisfaction is manifest. The law exercised by Principle is visible always. The gambler is demonstration or visibility of the action of Law. Law is op-

erating because of Principle. That God is the Principle and never recognizes actions which are not the manifestation of satisfaction, is self-evident.

48.   That Principle is One, is self-evident.

49.   That it is as much the religion of the gambler to gamble as for the preacher to preach is self-evident. That one and the same principle governs the orderly outcome of their ideas one by one is evident. It is as much the operation of the Principle of order that the preacher should smile in peace as that the thief should contort with anxiety.

50.   Each took his choice. Each experienced the logical outcome of his choice.

51.   Looking out at the skies at night what do we see? We say we see millions of stars. But we do not see stars. We see only memories of stars. Long ago the original stars ceased whose lights we behold.   Light is long in traveling to our sight. When it reaches us from a world long since gone we are watching memories. These shall suddenly depart from the skies of night. They shall roll away as a scroll.

52.   What do they stand for?

53.   They each stand for some great mind that thought along steadfast lines and looked to find God by the ways of thinking that study of God would bring God. Suddenly he knew that only by ceasing to expect to find God by any process of thinking or acting would he find God. He must be God to find God. The memory of his noble endeavor to find his good is the light of the stars. Nobody will see the night lights when the truth is told.

54. "Eye hath not seen nor ear heard." Neither hath it entered into the heart of man to conceive while he is thinking, that by the praise of an object he is coming nearer to his God. What he sees of God is that Principle is operating. The Principle is God. Principle spreads her wings over the thief and hurries him into his shame by her laws. Principle spreads her wings over the preacher and hurries him to his pale bed by her laws that as a man soweth, that shall he also reap.

55. He may reap anything but the satisfaction of Principle itself by carrying out the orderly sequence of his choice. He can reap satisfaction only by being satisfied.

56. If a mathematician at the board arranges that five and five shall be nine, his calculations will come out otherwise. That will be far from satisfaction. But they are as strictly the outcome of calculation as if he had said five and five are ten. He may get very brilliant in numbers, but he will never be satisfied. He shall stop thinking five and five are nine. He shall erase his figures. He shall stand at the center and start over again in truth.

57. The brilliant strength of his genius has now been secured by noble endeavor. It enables him suddenly to stop. It causes him to see, though nothing was gained by the calculation he has been practicing, he has gained all things by knowing that they are nothing. Now, without effort he knows the answer to his problems.

58. His journey over the roadway of effort has made him know without effort and do without effort.

59.   The third strength is the strength of doing without effort. The labor of Hercules should be performed without knowing that labor is being performed. To labor with effort is to go over the roadway of matter.

60.   The exercise thereof will leave the mind willing to stop laboring. The stoppage of effort is the line way of wisdom. To this mind the making visible of itself is the only work it does. It let its earth bring forth. It lets itself bring forth. There is a way of working that is efficient without strain.

61.   Jesus Christ had reference to this when he said. "Behold the lilies of the field, they toil not, neither do they spin."

62.   It was the sight of Jesus Christ the man that healed. Jesus did not strain and strive to do his works. He had gone over the whole roadway of human endeavor and found that it was nothing.

63.   Yet going over this roadway had given him authority to speak from experience.

64.   "The flesh profiteth nothing." To him the whole material universe was absent. Through the lines of every endeavor he saw the shining light of pure Principle streaming. Looking upon this stream was no effort. The men saw his face light with this stream and caught the true light and it healed them. "In thy light, we see light."

65.   Here looking into my face is the same illuminated face that glistened on the mount of transfiguration. It is the central fire of pure Principle. My eyes are not blinded by its light. Neither am I hidden by the night of the teachings of one who supposed that for the earth to bring forth it must labor.

66.   They shall not compel me to think that before I can preach the gospel I must have eloquent speech. They shall not make me think that before I can heal the sick I must study.   They shall not turn my mind away from Principle into the channel of supposing that I must be true and good by a process of penance before I can cast out demons. I must be strong in Spirit before I can raise the dead.

67.   All these works are done by my looking straight into thy face Jesus Christ, seeing Thee in the gambler as well as in the preacher—seeing Thee in the prizefight as well as the prayer room. For whoever has seen that there is only One Principle has no knowledge of any world except the One Spirit.

68.   There is no God—and all is God There is no Good—and all is Good There is no Life—and all is Life There is no Truth—and all is Truth There is no Love and—all is Love There is no Substance—and all is Substance There is no Intelligence—and all is Intelligence There is no Power—and all is Power.

69.   Only by throwing off all the God of the discussion of men and seeing into the face of the Principle that is the Fountain Head of all men, can God be found.

70.   This throwing off all God is the seeing of God. Seeing God is Being God.   I am always like what I see.

71.   I drop god that I may be God.

72.   I do not think that I may Think I do not live that I may Live I do not love that I may Love I do not move that I may Move I do not work that I may

Work I do not will that I may Will. I do not speak that I may Speak I do not create that I may Create.

73. I am meek and lowly of heart that I may be Omnipotent God.

74. Here at the poise between the knowledge that All is God and there is no God I begin my world over again. I blot out the past. I refuse the future. I bring forth what I am as I take my place in thy place. Henceforth there is no difference between Thee and me.

75. "I in Thee" and "Thou in me."

76. This is the bringing forth of my earth. The law is that it is faith that determines the quality of my efficiency. My faith is my poise of standing between my knowledge that now I am the Central Principle and all my thoughts are my choice, and the knowledge that all works are under the management of Principle, whether these come under the approval of mankind or under his disapproval.

77. Even the Principle of disapproval is God. The only Principle that operates is God.

78. All that is living and all that is Substance is Principle.

79. The thoughts that I think are my own. The world that I make is my own. Knowing this I shall cease to occupy my mind with condemnations of any line of endeavor. All lines are under the administration of Principle which knows them not. Principle knoweth only Itself.

80. I am Principle. Therefore I know myself. Knowing myself as Thyself is Jesus Christ. If there is only Jesus Christ there is no discord. In Me is peace.

81.   This Peace which I AM is governor of all the world. It is the poise of mind which regulates the thoughts of men.

82.   This is the God that "shall bring every work into judgment with every secret thing."

83.   Only the Principle by which all things operate shall endure.

84.   The things and their works are ceased by my silence, my peace.

85.   I am Principle.

There is not even the doctrine of freedom to be proclaimed. The highest is the unspeakable name into which the name Jesus Christ shall lead me. The unspeakable doctrine is the secret doctrine. I may not Be the secret doctrine till I have proclaimed freedom. I may not Be the openness of the secret doctrine till I have proclaimed freedom.

"Let us make man in our image, after our likeness: and let him have dominion." [Genesis 1:26]

LESSON ELEVEN

The Truth of Dominion

1.   It is related of a woman who lived alone in widowhood and extreme poverty that, after years of the most abject and pitiful prayers, noble petitions and strong appeals to the Omnipotent Jehovah, she suddenly changed her thoughts, shifted them as the wind shifts. Then her answer came—came as suddenly as her ideas had changed.

2.   Across the way from her miserable home a large cornfield had yearly waved its golden-topped harvest. Acres upon acres of corn yielded up their bounties to the millionaire owner of the cornfield every year. She would not have touched an ear of that corn. Her bringing up in the religion of her fathers had laid a great stress upon the sin of stealing. She would have shrunk back in horror and dismay at the idea of helping herself to the ears of corn.

3.   Suddenly, one day, after a prayer of exceeding power, after weary days without an answer to her petitions for assistance that she might not starve alone in her age and feebleness, the thought

came while she looked at the cornfield, "The earth is the Lord's and the fullness thereof."

4. "Then the cornfield over yonder is God's. He has spread it for My use. Year after year He has set it before Me and I would not eat of His bounty. So, I have been ungrateful and foolish." She went across the road and gathered some of her so-called neighbor's corn. She was content. A sense of gratitude fell into her heart like a drop of reviving wine. That very day a wonderful piece of good fortune came to her. From that time on she had no occasion to touch the ears of corn, for the long-delayed answer to her pitiful cry had come. She had set aside her one besetting sin—her most beclouding error. Can you name that error? It was her belief in stealing.

5. That command of Moses had passed down through the ages of her ancestors unmelted and untouched by the free Spirit of Jesus Christ, who had gone through the cornfields of his rich neighbors and known that as all was His Father's so all was His. It is nobler to think of Jesus Christ as replenishing the corn-ears because of His power than as fearing to touch them lest his neighbor be defrauded.

6. Long years of wrapped devotion in the worship of God had pressed the woman past the law into the Gospel. She had power now to replenish her neighbor's field; she must use it. For her there must be no law of defrauding, no law of stealing. She must be above the law, able to take the granules of matter and increase them by a new mode of using. She must use the cornfield as Jesus Christ used the cornfields—as master and owner, not as beggar and slave.

172

7. What great break from under the law must you make, My friend, to demonstrate that you are one with the Gospel of dominion, not under the law?

8. Notice—it was not license to steal—but knowing through the highly spiritual illumination—that there is only increase, there is no stealing that she was saved by.

9. It is written in the sacred books of nearly all the religions of the earth that it is by Divine word that the sick are most surely healed. This was the teaching and practice of Jesus Christ. But Jesus Christ was free born and free lived. He knew that a piece of clay is as much a Divine word as a word. That everything, even the words of men, when speaking the highest truths they know, is but a symbol of the Divine word which is the Spirit and Life. So he despised not the clay. He feared no symbol.

10. One of these who had been herself cured by the Divine Word alone, had made the words of Science her God. She had been prayerful, always strictly scientific, but set to the note that the words of Science as taught by her neighbors were God indeed, and Very God.

11. After a violent toothache when none of the words she had adored as her God would help, what seemed like insanity from pain took possession. Suddenly she called for a hot drink. It was given. Instantly the pain ceased. The tooth quieted. Months passed, the year sped, yet she says the tooth has never given the slightest sign of its enmity to her since. She signed her freedom from the worship of words with that break. No pain, no sick-

sickness, no trouble in the physical, have been out of the reach of her words in her family since.

12. The moment her worship of the words as any more God in themselves than the hot drink was God in itself, ceased, she was free—let loose as the bird from the snare of the fowler.

13. What had her hours and days and months of scientific denial and affirmation brought her? They had brought her face to face with her thick and foolish belief in matter. To break from matter she must know so strongly that there is no matter, that she could use matter and not hate nor fear it.

14. What do you hate and fear beyond all things? It seems like a virtue in your eyes. It is not a virtue. It is a belief in two powers, two substances, two kinds of surroundings. Drop your prejudices. Drop your hating. Drop fearing lest you do wrong. Be free as you were born. Does this mean that you will defile yourself and your reputation? No, it means that you are cleansed from defilement.

15. Who shall be stopped out of the reach of the law? Shall it be those who have broken the law through despising the law? No, it means that they shall be above the law who have yielded honorable obedience to the law. Only those whom Christ hath set free are free indeed. Only those who do not know any law never break any law. Only those who are above the law because they know the freedom of the Spirit never break the law.

16. Such do not neglect their families simply to gratify selfish whims of pure mortality. They entirely protect and provide for their families by the bounty and goodness of the Spirit. Such do not ne-

glect to pay their just dues to show out their independence of matter, but Spirit is bountiful and noble through them.

17. The woman came up out of the law into the freedom of the Gospel by prayer—not through love of sensation into the license of defiance of law. Let there be the freedom of Christ—not the license of Nero.

THERE ARE TWENTY-FOUR ELDERS

18. Twelve of these are the first lessons in Spiritual Science concerning the management of the universe by the word of denying that there is any universe to manage. And twelve of these elders are the absolution from the necessity for words. There are no words with which to work and no necessity for words. This is the mission of the twelve elders at the right of the throne. They also fall down on their faces when God as pure freedom, pure holiness, pure ignorance of law and Gospel takes His seat in the heart.

19. To be ignorant of the law through knowing the law in meek obedience there unto, is to be absolutely free from knowledge of law.

20. To be cheated and beaten by neighbors through ignorance of their nature as human and ignorance of their nature as Spirit is darkness. To be protected from cheatings and lyings of neighbors by the law of the word that there is no power can touch one while God is on his side, is to be set free by the law of the Spirit of Truth. The keeping of this doctrine faithfully passes us on into the hands of the next teachings of Science where there is no law of the Spirit.

21.   It is the reiteration of the second set of truths which makes us deaf and blind and sense-less to evil which is the taking the throne of God in the Soul I must arrive into. I must be blind and deaf and dumb and senseless to evil, not through ignorance and defiance of law, but through knowl-edge of and obedience unto law. No man cometh unto the throne save he before whom the twenty-four lessons are mastered so that there is no need of them, but only use of them.

22.   Jesus replenished the corn by plucking it. Jesus increased the riches of the owners of the swine by running them into the sea. This was by knowing that God cannot steal. This was by know-ing himself as God. When I come through obedi-ence of the law into the liberty of the sons of God it will be a help to you to take my goods. We shall have all things in common.   We shall know that there is no taking from nor adding to, no helping no hurting.

ALL IS ONE

23.   Moses is teaching of the Spirit of Man as the Spirit of   God—free—foolish—ignorant— "And God said: 'Let us make man in our image and let him have dominion.'"

24.   Fools for Christ's sake and the Gospel are one with God. Ignorance through the Wisdom of God is freedom with Christ.

25.   Man is the rising of the Jesus Christ to be master of the elders.   Jesus Christ takes the throne of the Soul as knowing neither the highest law nor the highest Gospel.

26.   Jesus Christ is exalted above virtue and goodness. High out of the reach of principalities

and powers is the Owner of the Soul, the Mind, the Spirit. "Let us make," said Goodness and Virtue, "Him that shall have dominion." So with the virtuous law and Gospel of goodness, obeyed in meekness the Holy One of Israel arose Very God of Very God.

27.   He now arises in my Soul, my Spirit, my Mind, Jesus Christ who condescends to be me and transcends me!

28.   "Let us make," said Faith and Hope, "the will." God as faith and hope stirs the soul with flying powers as the wings of a bird move. The Faith of God is God. The Hope of God is God. The Will of God is the face of God.

29.   When Faith and Hope stir the mind the will faces the universe with its own decrees and sees its own kingdom according to its own choice.

30.   As the two wings of a bird carry its face into sight of the glorious home of its heart, so Hope and Faith, the two wings of the Soul, carry its will into sight of its Home.

31.   Dominion is the birthright of Mind over matter. Dominion is the birthright of will over mind. Dominion is the birthright of Spirit over the will. Dominion is the birthright of God over the spirit. Dominion is the birthright of Jesus Christ over God.

For God is the only power. "God visible is the only God."

32.   To be ignorant of law is darkness.   To be ignorant of the Gospel is darkness still. To be ignorant of the law through the Gospel is the light of knowledge.   To be ignorant of the Gospel through

Jesus Christ is Life and Immortality made visible or brought to light. It is the bringing into sight of Myself as I AM which is my God made visible.

33. "God said, Let us make man and let him have dominion"

34. Not till by my Hope and Faith absolutely filling and moving me am I moved, can I see my Home. I must open my eyes on the kingdom of my dominion arranged for me from the foundation of God. I can only do this as Jesus Christ. The Kingdom is to be seen only by him who through obedience to law is above the law—who through the bringing of the Gospel is free from the Gospel. He can see the Kingdom of the Absolute.

35. God would not be great unless He could condescend. God would not be mighty unless He could transcend. He would not be able except He could be visible as Friend, Companion, Counselor, King, Champion.

36. The texts of Moses have more and more uncovering energy. If one sees that this eleventh movement of the wheel of the law is only a masterful Deity taking physical or supernatural hands and forming a man and a woman that is one plane of thought. The man and the woman so formed shall seem to be the one who imagines that a Great Being did make a physical, visible pair—full of pride and conceit — full of wrangling competition. They shall have brokenness of hopes and brokenness of faith because they shall see hope and faith as human and fallible like the bodies and minds of the pair.

37. If one rises beyond this idea of the meaning of Moses and thinks it is the Spiritual nature God

is forming, he may tell us how this spiritual nature has man and woman to initiate it, and they are filled with ignorance of the power of the Spirit. He may speak of man and woman to initiate it, and they are filled with the Spirit—too willful in error to hear the command that to man is given dominion. It will seem to this interpreter of the text as if in his closet mankind had accused this world of foolishness and ignorance in relation to Spirit and had thereby surrounded himself with two kinds of experiences—good and bad.

38.   But there is no power of accusing given to Himself by the Omnipotent Jehovah.   To the only Power, the only Wisdom, the only Judgment, there is no self-accusation, and thus there is no accusation of His creations.

39.   It is the Perfect Mind that takes of its own Substance, Virtue, and Goodness—Hope and Faith —and by their uniting exposed Himself to His world.

40.   Hope and Faith make the Will manifest. Jesus Christ is the Will of God manifest. The Will is the Word made flesh and dwelling among us. The flesh is God made visible. Jesus Christ is the making of God visible. To Jesus Christ there is no decay. Thus the flesh that is Truth is immortal Beauty.   To Jesus Christ there is no Death. Thus the true flesh formed by the uniting of Hope and Faith is immortal life.

41.   The visible Man formed by Virtue and Goodness is Spirit.   This is the true flesh.   This is the formation of the Man of Dominion.

42.   The still higher interpretation of the text is that there is no Virtue and Goodness out of which

to form the Will of the Spirit. There is no God out of which to make men and there is no dominion belonging to man because there is nothing to have dominion over—that the very idea of dominion is error. The idea of dominion is translated into the idea of being ruled over as well as ruling over.

43. There is no knowing which way the idea will swing its strength through the mind: whether it shall cause man to feel he is lauded over by his fellow men or whether he shall think he lauds it over them. If he thinks they laud it over him his life is rebellious yielding. This is not obedience to a Truth but obedience to an error. He wears the marks of a slave in his face.

44. If anybody's will has come down into my face telling me that I must not do this and I must not do that, I wear the mark of a slave. My flesh shows forth the marks of having been beaten against my will. If this idea has come down received by Me as that I have the right to say to my neighbor that he must or must not do as I command, all my neighbors wear the faces of slaves and their darkness hardens and blackens my face till I am more slave than they.

There is no right given me to tell you what you shall or shall not do. I may not tell you that if you sin you will die. This is the doctrine of let thy neighbor go free. Give way to this rightful dominion. His dominion is freedom. That is the only dominion there is. Give me my freedom. I give thee thy freedom. This is the doctrine of Will. This is the word of Moses. This is Jesus Christ. If the Mormon is let go free by my mind taking off its yoke of abhorrence from his neck, he will let his wives go free. They will not bring forth children under bond-

under bondage. They will bring forth thoughts of God whose white wings shall fold me round with clothing of beauty.

45. If I take my yoke of abhorrence of lies off the business dealings of the world, I shall set businessmen free to be honest. They will set their customers free from their yokes and their customers being themselves free will never employ children or animals to work under their orders. They shall think thoughts of sweetness that shall come to me and I shall eat them with refreshment.

46. If I take my yoke of abhorrence from the rum seller, he will let his customers go free from his clutch on their will; and they being free will raise into the skies to drop down fair lights on my Soul to be bright in the Lord.

47. But this text of Moses has even more splendid light in its wings for the earth.

48. There is not even the doctrine of freedom to be proclaimed. The highest is the unspeakable name into which the name Jesus Christ shall lead me. The unspeakable doctrine is the secret doctrine. I may not be the secret doctrine till I have proclaimed freedom. I may not be the openness of the secret doctrines till I have proclaimed freedom.

49. I must take off my yoke of abhorrence from Satan that there may be seen freedom from Satan in all my world. I must take off my abhorrence from vice that there may be no vice in all the fields of Omnipresence. I must take off my yoke of abhorrence from slavery that there may be no slavery.

50. The belief that there is a God ruling over Me is the origin of slavery. Even God shall have no dominion in my creed.

51.   God is freedom from dominion. God is freedom from the idea of dominion. God is freedom from the mind capable of holding the idea of dominion. God is ALL. Therefore there is no mind holding the idea of dominion.

52.   To lose the idea of dominion is to lose the idea of freedom. This is the secret doctrine open freely to him who receives it in truth by giving his God and his neighbor absolute freedom.

53.   Does the idea of freedom remind me of bondage? Must I not then lose even my idea of freedom before I am one with Him who is above freedom?

54.   Does not the idea of virtue remind Me of vice? Must I not lose even my idea of virtue before I am one with Him who is above Virtue?

55.   Moses caught sight of Him who is above freedom. He said all the time "Let." This word has the potentiality of hosts of archangels.

56.   It is the breaking down of an atmosphere of mind thin but tough as the atmosphere that hides the earth from the falling stars. The atmosphere of piety which makes the children fear to act roughly, the odor of sanctity that keeps the young from going astray—these make an aura about the heads of the saints which keep them from the oneness with God their prayers are beseeching. Why should their atmosphere check the freedom of the children by telling them without words that they were intending to do wrong or might be getting into error?

57.   Are not the children as white as their elders? Who set any mark of authority to restrain upon them or any? Nobody.

58. He who shall dwell in order of sanctity, compelling by his presence, is the restraint of a human will. He is an infinite believer in evil. When the effect of his silent dominion is lost there is the belief of license.

59. Sanctity/License—this is the swing of the pendulum of mind.

60. The one who has folded himself about with virtue and goodness as a garment, keeps the prayers of his lifetime from coming to fruitage. He pushes the freedom of many to the very walls and their yoke is his yoke. Many a good and pious heart wonders with infinite wonder why his prosperities do not come, when all his world regards him as worthy. He is wrapped around with a belief in goodness as with a garment of impenetrable ether. Through this garment of belief the prosperous goods of open toleration of all things will not flow.

To believe in goodness is to believe in badness. The terribly good will wonder why the terribly bad have the goods of the world. The terribly good is in ignorance that the terribly bad do not believe in their own badness as intolerably as he believes in it. They that let the world come and go without the wisdom thereof, do more wisely in thinking things are none of their business than the good who feels the responsibility of converting them.

61. The saint is wrapped around with the ether of foolishness. The sinner is wrapped around with the earth soils of foolishness. It is all a belief in matter and evil.

62. The doctrine of "Let be" for the saint would open the sluice-ways of heaven to pour down the gold and frankincense and myrrh.

63. The doctrine of "Let be" held as a principle of goodness by the sinner would change him in the twinkling of an eye, transform him into his first estate. He would be melted into the clear Spirit of God.

64. The doctrine of "Let be" held in ignorance is higher than the doctrine of "I bind you to my ideas," in the supposition, "I am holier than thou."

65. So the virtuous may take no credit to himself, and the saint-like may not boast in his soul, for prosperity cannot reach them till they have reached some star in the heavens where virtue is not worshipped and goodness is not made an idol of.

66. There they will see that God hath made of one blood all nations. There is none evil nor good. They are all one in Jesus Christ.

67. The Unity of God is the Unity of Jesus Christ with Man and God. All men and Jesus Christ and these twain and God make One. To hold this in peace is to find wisdom speaking forth from all things. The rocks shall be seen by their words. The flies and the cherubim shall be found neither higher nor lower.

68. The weariness of the yoke of one seeming more intelligent than another rises into buoyant vigor where ever the mind sifts its fine glory of "Let be". "Let be" is the making of Wisdom. "Let be" is making manifest of Substance. LET BE is the making manifest of Health.

Man is the coming forth into sight of the word of the highest Let Be. The fine sifting white Substance of "Let it be done" is pouring from many today. Watch its streaming with fiercer and stronger glory! It is the knowledge that there is none but the offspring and wisdom of Omniscience. Knowing this and resting in the peace of pure knowing is the hastening baptism of Wisdom. By this baptism we are lifted away from thinking any doctrine too high for the people.

69.   From thence forward none shall come into our presence but the speakers of Wisdom. For there is none to come while the freedom of Mind is Let Be and the abhorrence of folly is lost.

70.   It is the doctrine of "LET BE" which gives man the visibility of the Word.

71.   By this freedom from virtue and freedom from goodness the idea of Spirit held by the mind that has not known that these are not truth, drops from the mind.

72.   The man of Spirit imagined by the lovers of virtue and goodness is not the true man to the mind that has let drop its ideas of virtues and goodness knowing these to be bondage wherever he walks.

73.   The age of extreme religious sanctity and much checking of freedom is always followed by the license of immodesty and indulgence.

74.   Thus the bondage of all belief is apparent. It is not Omniscience to believe anything. It is Omniscience to believe all things. It is not Omnipotence to be powerful and dominant. It is Omnipotence to be the only Power. It is not Omnipresence to give instruction to mankind as to what

to do and what not to do. It is Omnipresence to "Let BE" and thus make manifest Man, the Idea and demonstration of One Presence.

Omnipresent Omnipotent Omniscient

When I find the World starving for the words that will revive the heart and satisfy the judgment, I will finish the starvation by a doctrine that will feed and entrance with joyous fulfillment.

"In Thy Presence is the fullness of Joy." [Psalms 16:11]

"For in Him dwelleth all the fullness of the Godhead bodily." [Colossians 2:9]

LESSON TWELVE

The Finished Work

1.   Michelangelo was once asked to criticize some of Raphael's frescoing. He said nothing, but took a crayon and drew a figure the best he could, and said: "I criticize by example."

2.   Mendelssohn once said: "I do not want to hear so much criticism of music. I want the critic to compose some music."

3.   There is a mighty truth we start out with now.   It is this: We are the artificers and finishers of the fate of empires.   We are the majestic power by reason of that thinking faculty by which we crystal out our world in which we walk.

4.   If I, myself, made the Russian Siberia with its cold, its putrid fish, its exiles, by my peculiar thoughts of limitations of the rights of mankind, I will finish up these things by taking the Jesus Christ offer of an open door which no man can shut.   I will construct a new Siberia by thinking of my Father's Kingdom of plenty and beauty and delight.   Thus Siberia shall be finished and built, and

the former stretch of Northern waste shall bloom with the splendors of Arcadia.

5. When Jesus Christ found a multitude of men and women and children hungry, he finished their hunger by feeding them. When the sun finds the rose waiting for warmth, he finishes its waiting hope by fulfillment. When I find the world starving for the words that will revive the heart and satisfy the judgment, I will finish the starvation by a doctrine that will feed and entrance with joyous fulfillment. When I find the youth and vigor of the world dropping into graves of despair under the cold night of truthful praises I will redden the cheeks of my people and quicken their steps with swift brightness. When Jesus Christ found the nations sick for long-deferred freedom he took off their yoke and forth from their springs of freedom there sprang abounding health.

6. I am the keeper of the doctrine of Jesus Christ. In heaven and in earth and under the earth where matter has forged its delusions around and about the creatures of nature, my voice is heard proclaiming that, "Now is come salvation and the Kingdom of my God and my Christ." This is the end of empires. This is the creation of heaven. If I may choose which world I may walk in, I will choose the world of God. If I may bespeak who shall be my companions through the immortal spaces of life, I will bespeak princes of knowledge and goodness, and sisters of beauty and wisdom.

7. If I have, by my imaginations of things that are not true concerning the nature of the creation of God, made a company of Italian beggars, Arctic exiles, and Chinese slaves, I will put an end to this swarm of creatures by my Knowledge in which

there is no mixture of imagination of lies. I will crystal out of the white Substance of God my earth of entrancing delight. I will warm forth the roses of Sharon slumbering under the cold darkness of my superstitions which I have taught, that God ordained the poor to be with me and the miserable to cry near me forever. I know that it is by the voice of the Lord in the Garden of Spirit that Adam shall be ashamed and shall hide his face from my face forever. Adam is the supposition, the naming, of that which is opposite to Spirit. "The earth is clean dissolved before me," said Isaiah.

8. Let matter roll away as a dream. Let Adam be hidden in the brightness of Christ. There is the loud voice of God speaking today: "Adam, where art thou?" And Adam from this day doth know that in Paradise he is supplanted by Jesus. He walketh no more who claimeth the name of dust. He is finished who called himself mortal. He that called himself Spirit is seen in his beauty and wisdom.

9. The troops of redeemed walking in white on the highways of Eden are singing the songs of the Lamb in my hearing. They are not invisible to me because I am not of the race of Adam; I am of the race of Christ. Standing on the mountain of light where the feet of the Lord are sandalled in truth, I choose to be true. I know all the story of Adam to be but a fable. I know all the history of materiality to be but a dream. I know all the law of creation of earth and its inhabitants by thoughts to be but the simple thought in my mind of wisdom as to what would be here and what would be there if I as the Infinite God were not all.

10.   If I tell myself that X is the value of my Immortal Soul I am not by that speech thinking that X is the value, but am letting myself suppose myself to be nothing; and by beginning at the foundation of Being, I am able to take of this tree of knowledge of truth and imagination which Moses calls the tree of good and evil, and still live on as Immortal Soul, knowing its value in God and knowing its value in Adam.

I have no quarrel with the church for telling me that I fell from my first estate of truth and glory by eating of the tree of knowledge of good and evil. I know that in Adam all is imagination—that in Christ all is understanding. I know that it is not a dangerous thing for me to be told that it is not true that I imagined the error that there is another beside myself. I did not imagine that I was another creation unlike Myself. I put down the proposition as a mathematician would let X equal the price of the corn. As the student of numbers would be no wise to his own judgment if he should think that X were really the price of the corn, so I should not be worth while to myself in my own estimation if I should think of Myself as letting the mortal really represent Me. I am not the mortal. I do not think that the mortal represents Me. I tell Myself that at every step of My spirit the mortal is its simulation in some way or another.

11.   If I am joyous of heart, the mortal, My opposite, is weeping with pain. If I say I am wise and full of understanding, the mortal that represents Me whines because it cannot tell whence it came forth and is wholly unable to tell the laws of its life. If I am speaking of power and greatness, the mortal is telling of being under bondage of fear and whim-

pering because its neighbors have gotten on ahead. But the misery of the mortal does not affect Me, the appearance of bondage does not bring Me into chains.

12.   If I am speaking in Spirit of My thoughts as strong in their ability to bring into My sight the noblest of beings, My mortal representative may that moment be whining that its associates are all poor and unlearned.

13.   I will speak one word to My mortal X who typifies Me, which he shall never get away from. I will call him by a name which shall be My name. If then he will speak forth the name I will give him, he shall escape all the ills of the flesh.   If he refuses to speak forth from that name, I will let him take such life as his speaking against his own name will mean.

14.   I will call him Ananaias. This shall be truly My name put upon him. He shall be My Grace. Under all circumstances his talismanic world shall be his own name, the name I have put in his forehead. It shall always be: "My grace is sufficient for thee."   I shall put near it its shadow. That shadow shall be the fear of coming to want.   In Truth if he will turn to the light as the roses smile in the sun, he will speak the word that I put in his forehead and smilingly whisper My name. "My Grace is sufficient for thee."   It shall be My voice ever speaking these words when he speaks.

Then he may give of his gold to the church; he may donate his banks to the schools; he may turn over his goods to the saints, but he shall still have riches beyond riches. I am his giver. He need never earn his living. He need never look ahead for his patrimony. He is born to the gifts of free Grace.

But on the other hand he may turn to the shadow—the opposite of My name as the planets wheel into their nights—and fear that he shall come into want through My not providing his living. Then he may speak forth some lie. His one fault shall be that he is always making himself out to be poorer than he really is. He is forever telling how little money he has—is that one in whose forehead I have put promise that while he tells of My gifts and praises My bounty, attributing all his success and possessions to Me, he shall be rich. He shall utterly depend for his riches upon the truth he tells Me. When he lies by complaining even in the simplest fashion to his neighbors concerning his lacks—his needs—his wants—he shall lose his riches step by step or all in a mass. He shall go the way of his word, for it is My pleasure as the Principle of Truth to make a word the arbiter of a man's destiny, in the mortal.

15. The mortal that keeps still while the Spirit is speaking of Me and the name I have set in its place shall decline and be gone. It shall let the light of Myself shine down over its place.

16. The mortal has the appearance of choosing. Its choosing is only to choose not to speak. The mortal tendeth to shadow. It tendeth to lies. It longeth to speak of its troubles. In its Scriptures it speaketh of itself as full of troubles and "prone to err as the sparks fly upward." It has poetry and song. Scripture and science are full of the sorrowful teachings of My dealings.

17. But all the time each man and each woman has My name written in his forehead, and if they

will speak that name it shall act as a talisman of enchantment; they shall rise out of the sight of the pains of the flesh.

18. To one I am written in his forehead as "God is with me." To another I am written in his forehead as "Freedom." To another I am written as "Prophecy and Sound Judgment" To another I am "The morning star of overcoming new pleasures." These names are written in all the foreheads of all sentient creatures. And by each one's side dropping under his feet I forever put the name of the opposite of the true name. I also will choose their delusions," saith the Lord. So I also, the God of Spiritual man have told plainly what is his opposite in name and character and office.

19. I know when I Myself by My true name, unspeakable by the voice who has not known his own name and held it till the simulation, the shade of his name has been lost as mine has been lost. Whoever shall lose his mortal name, as mine is lost, him I know I shall find the companion and friend of Myself.

20. Whoever speaks his own name that I, creator of the Spiritual man, have put in his forehead, shall feel the opposite state of affairs, from the nature I breathe on his being, melt into absence. All shades of evil—all claims of hardships—shall fade from his mind, from his life, from his substance, from his pathway. Then he shall stand naked in God. He shall be one with Jesus Christ, who was the first of My thought, with the naming of evil. Whoever refused to be governed by evil, He shall have My name without any naming of evil. Whoever has refused to be governed by evil, He shall have My name without any naming of the mortal—

without any semblance of substance—without any deception, of hurt, or ignorance. His name that I put in his forehead shall be his own, his right to his place—his with which to start out untrammeled to wander over the fields of the country where I dwell.

21.   If that one whose name is "God is with Me"— Emmanuel—lets the mortal speak, his one cry shall be, "I am alone," till he rise boldly against it. That is his temptation. Yet I will never let him that hears this name be tempted to speak on the shade side of that name above so that he is able to speak boldly, "God is with Me." He shall go from honor to honor, from riches to riches, by speaking My name.

22.   In the presence of the signs of bondage, the trials of conditions imposed by others, as it shall seem, the mind that has My name as "Freedom" written in its center shall speak boldly, "I am Free" I will never let temptation to bondage get darker than the power of that word in his speaking.

23.   To him who has My name written on his forehead as "Prophecy and Sound Judgment" I will never let the seemings of evil to come upon him get out of the reach of the power of his own prophecy of Good for himself in the judgment based on implanted knowledge of Me. He shall never forebode evil unto himself. He shall bravely rise up from such temptation and prophesy loudly and strongly of good to come. Then it shall be plain in his sight that his seeming burden of evil to come was nothing—nothing but phantasm, the shade of a name. His glory among his people shall be his great judgment and his power of foretelling the good that is waiting for all of his neighbors. As My prophet he

he shall go from strength to strength. He shall have letters without having learned.

24. I will put My name as the Light Bringer into the forehead of one. He shall speak wisdom as easily as the breath he breathes. Yet to his neighbors he shall often seem to speak folly. He shall have temptations to say that which puts him in disfavor. If he shall say, "I am right because in My spirit I am the Light of the World," he shall find himself always the illumination and charm of his world. On all themes he shall have light.

Nothing of truth can be hidden from him, and none can mistake his meanings when he speaks of the Spirit. He shall never speak of himself as ignorant. He shall be Lucifer, Sun of the Morning, never believing in darkness, never agreeing with ignorance. I will never let the claims of his temptations to think he is not wise get out of reach of his light that he is wise. Then at much recounting of My praise as Light—as Wisdom—as Judgment—he shall go from light to light. He may converse with the stars. He may counsel with the beings who travel on missions of light over the highways of Eden.

25. Thus I have named all the people of the earth. Thus are you named. At the height of your speaking you shall see that Adam, the sense side— the shade side—the seeming—is nothing, pure nothing. From the first your deepest sorrows were nothing. They were not put there for you to overcome, but to declare phantoms in fearless rejections.

26. I chose your delusions. I named the opposite of your true nature. It walks and runs and

leaps with your moving, but it may drop out of your sight as the shades fall from the towers when the noon strikes their tips. You need not overcome the seeming opposite in your nature—you may only know that it is delusion—is but your own peculiar shade—the temptation in the garden to listen to Satan, who whispers that if you speak to yourself as mortal it shall not bring unto you mortal conditions.

But Satan is silent on the theme that the Christ speaks so boldly forth. Satan does not tell you that "The flesh profiteth nothing"—that is speaking only of what might be if the good were not all—if I were not the only Substance. Satan is silent when he tells you that in the day you eat of the knowledge of evil you shall not die. He is right to say you shall not die. For there is nothing in you to die. You are like Me. You may know that in the mortal you are nothing—in My name you are all.

27.   This is the twelfth fruit of the tree of life. Moses spake it forth and its goodness and beauty are now waiting the eating of all mankind.   It is the doctrine that I, as God, know all My works of My hands as good. I know the name I have set in your forehead is Good. You know it is good.   The moment you speak that the work of My hands is good, that moment you know yourself as I made you.

28.   You know that you are Me. You see that My name is your name.   You do not speak evil or darkness of yourself. It is now that "God sees all the work of His hands as Good." This is the Infinite, Ineffable Light.

29.　This is the last "LET BE" of the truth. From this moment there is no delusion that hath name. The truth only brings forth.

30.　If to mankind I am the only Substance, his thoughts shall from henceforth be brought forth and multiplied in perfection. There shall only honor and sweet fame and fair successes crown the name of him who often repeats the name I have put in his forehead. He shall be crowned with the laurels of fame. Yet fame shall be only the honor of My name in the sound of his ears. The greatness of his name shall be in his heart only the sweetness of My name.

31.　This is your honor upon whom I have put My name—that it is in Me that you glory. If any man boast he shall boast in the name of his God— the God of Truth, all pride taken unto yourself as on the line of Adam or shade side shall come to naught.　Its portion shall be the grave. But of him who is true in the sight of all to the name I put in his life, the name of his goodness that shall live in memory of man through all the ages—as Moses, Abraham, Enoch now live.

32.　As the science of Moses is understood, I shall be found to be the only science; I shall seem to be the name of all science. Then there shall be the true church upon the earth known and under- stood of all mankind. All men shall be known to themselves.　Alone with Me you shall feel yourself companioned with the great in the presence of lofty comrades. Men shall not ask favors of their neigh- bors. They shall not need to be favored. In himself each one shall be satisfied in Me. I am his favor. He must have himself to his own friendship. I think his name, and he shall think. This is the work of man. Jesus has finished his work. "My Father worketh hereto and I work." My work, as Father and Origin—First cause and Creator is thinking. I think, and man thinks. He thinketh My thoughts with Me. He thinketh the name I put in his forehead. This is the beginning of Wisdom. This is the beginning of Glory. This is the beginning of his bringing-forth power. When he thinks the truth of Me and himself, man shall say, "My work of My thoughts is Good." He shall see that his thoughts of good are all that come to fruitage.

33.   It is the highest elder of the elders round about My throne who teaches that the wrath of man shall praise him who speaks the name I have in his forehead. Do you believe with all your mind that, when you are accused of lying, it shall help make the glory of your fame and your name? If you do, then you have learned the twenty-fourth lesson of the Science of God. The twenty-fourth elder has fallen down in your presence satisfied of your knowledge of Me. Do you believe that when you are accused of cheating and adultery, then is the time when your honor is beginning to shine with greater and clearer brightness upon the earth and among the stars because My presence is sufficient strength and medicine for our name? Then the twenty-fourth turn of the wheel of Science is made and you do not need any further instructions. Fear thou not upon the earth, whatsoever thy name, when thou knowest thyself safe in My keeping. "The sun shall not smite thee by day nor the moon by night."

34.   The temptations of praise and the greatness of kindness shall not turn thee out of thy course. The stars of the night—which are igno-

rance of the shame of the hateful, shall not hide their smiles. Thou art setting thy foot on thy throne with Me. Dost thou think that it is not necessary in the demonstration of thy Divinity and thine own greatness to have trouble and affliction to make thee good and upright and noble? Thou art right. Thou hast learned this—the twenty-fourth lesson of Science—the twelfth lesson of the Gospel of Christ.

35. The last and subtlest temptation laid into thy path is to be tempted to think that, in order to be great, the saints must be purified by pain, by shame, by humiliation. The finest shade of the delusion of semblance is the claim that a saint will only glow in the beauty of goodness with the wheels of affliction turned upon him.

36. It was not because Jesus was accused of being a glutton, a wine-bibber and a companion of thieves and harlots that his name shines as the sun in the firmament of splendors, but because these things were known as nothing. Their true side was visible to him from the first. He did not need purifying. He was already fine as the white gold of My substance. He did not need purifying. He was already pure as the light of My love. Neither do you need trying to find out the stuff you are made of. You were made of Me from the beginning. You are fine as gold of My white Being. You do not need purifying. You are pure as My Spirit—pure as the crystal fires in which I bathed you on the morn of Creation.

37. If you refuse the message of the retiring Adam, whose greatest glory is to be refined out of sight—that you have to be tried to humiliation and sorrow, then you understand Truth in its last deal-

ing with Adam. Your first philosophy teaches that the Gods make you great by keeping you humiliated. This is the refinement of error. It is not true. I am not honored in you or by your shame. I do not chasten you to make you great. It was your nature with Me before the world was, to be great. It is your nature now to be noble. Nothing can alter it. But it is the demonstration, the visibility, the face of My name in your face, when these last temptations of the delusions I named are looked out of sight by the Truth of your life.

38.   Everything evil shall melt in your presence. Everything hard shall fade in your sight. As pure water unmixed by dross, will dissolve the stones, the iron pipes, the lead pipes, the sand, the diamond, so the purity of the motive, the crystal water of thy fair purpose, shall dissolve thine enemies, dissolve thy defamations, dissolve the shame and the shamers out of the memory of mind. Nothing can hold against purity. Speak thou the name I have put in thy forehead. That is thy secret between thee and Me. Ask counsel of no man—I am thy Wisdom. Ask help of no man—I am thy helper. Ask friendship of no man—I am thy friend. Thy healing way is thine own way—I am thy Healer. Thy work is My work—I am thy worker. There is none can call in question the Beauty and Perfection of thy work—I am It. I am the Fame and Splendor of thy work.

39.   Be satisfied with thy work. I am satisfied with My work. Art thou satisfied with thy work? If thou art not satisfied with thy work thou hast not received the twelfth lesson of the law. Thou hast not touched the heights of the twelfth lesson of the Gospel. The twelfth lesson of the law of the word is

to say: "I am satisfied with the work of My mind." The twelfth lesson of the Gospel is to be satisfied with My work as the finished work—it is seeing My finished work in the faces of all men.

40.   Dost thou see My face in all faces? Then thou art taking thy seat on thy throne with Me.

41.   I am the Maker of all that is made and My work is finished. Seeing Myself in all My own universe I am in blessed delight. "In Me is fullness of joy." He who sees Me in all things smiling forth is past the use of the lessons of God. Wherever he walks he is the lesson of God.

42.   The first six lessons of the Gospel are self-evident truths. The last six lessons of the Gospel are the use of those truths in the world. They make the world a heaven to walk in. "Let us hear the conclusion of the whole matter." All the delusions of Adam are the formless fear of the protoplasm. All feeling of fear or dread is the origin of the protoplasmic void of matter as it first appears. All naming of fear is the amoeba that springs into hurt or trouble, deceiving mankind to seem real.

43.   All things and all actions are equally under the law of cause and effect, of logical outcome, and are, therefore, under one Principle only. The thief is acting out the logic of his ideas; so is the saint. The logic is the "I am Ruler" whose Nature is Me. The beauty of the Gospel is that it is wisdom to be foolish as to stealing and lies—for I am the Substance that takes nothing but increases all. I can speak only Truth. I am telling the truth when I as Satan tells, that to taste of knowledge of evil is not death. For I know that mortality is nothing and has no power to die. I chose the delusion of Satan. His

logical sequence is Me. The logic of all things is Me. So I am All and in all and there is nothing but Me. I am Principle. I am the logic of actions. I am the sequence of Words. I am the Science of all things. I am Omniscience Ineffable!

44.　　My name is written deep in all things, meekly waiting to speak of their name in the Light of My Love. The time for their speaking has come. I will that they all shall speak now. Gather thou into thy speaking nothing but glory. Work out this glory without the naming of evil or good. In harmony of music, in beauty of art, see only My strokes of love. So shall the Spirit of Inspiration of Raphael—of Michelangelo—of Mendelssohn—come into the voices and features and forms of all nature. To the pure I am seen.

45. By them that in the heart of their thoughts I am only felt, the Spirit of Love and Light shall be seen. They shall walk with Me in white, for they are worthy of My name through speaking My name.

I, Jesus, AM GOD.

Guidelines for Daily Practice

Emma recommended a daily practice and offered general guidelines for living in accordance with our highest selves, as follows:

1. Be cheerful under all circumstances; to be cheerful is to be praise-full.

2. Sit down at a certain time every day and write down on paper what your idea of Good is. Write the highest ideas of Good you have...such a practice will pin you down to the truth and it is in Truth that there is power

3. Take two of the 12 doctrines (lessons) and repeat them each day. Spend an hour in the morning reasoning out the lessons that address your own nature (lessons 1-6) and an hour in the afternoon on lessons addressing the people around you and your environment (your ministry—lessons 7-12).

4. By going over and over the lessons we come nearer the healing feeling. Use this book or *Scientific Christian Mental Practice* or *High Mysticism* as a starting point for your focused time; meditate on the material and your experiences; act accordingly.

The goal is always to move to a deeper understanding, with an intellectually satisfying line of reasoning and an emotional/intuitive feeling underlying the possibility being considered. With these, the practitioner is sure to experience the "thrill of cool fire" that lets one know that the hidden power, latent in all of us, is working to show us the Good.

Other Books by Emma Curtis Hopkins

- Class Lessons of 1888 (WiseWoman Press)
- Bible Interpretations
- Esoteric Philosophy in Spiritual Science
- Genesis Series
- High Mysticism
- Judgment Series in Spiritual Science
- Resume (WiseWoman Press)
- Scientific Christian Mental Practice (DeVorss)

Books About Emma Curtis Hopkins

- Emma Curtis Hopkins, Forgotten Founder of New Thought – Gail Harley
- Unveiling Your Hidden Power: Emma Curtis Hopkins' Metaphysics for the 21st Century – Ruth L. Miller
- Unveiling Your Hidden Power Practice Guide – Ruth L. Miller

To find more of Emma's work, including some previously unpublished material, log on to:

www.emmacurtishopkins.org

WISEWOMAN PRESS

2850 SW Cedar Hills Blvd #65
Beaverton, Oregon 97005
800.603.3005
www.wisewomanpress.com

FORTHCOMING BOOKS

by Emma Curtis Hopkins

Resume

Self Treatments

by Ruth L. Miller

A Book of Uncommon Prayer

Notre Dame: Mary Magdalene & the Divine Feminine

Living A New Dream

150 Years of Healing: The Founders and Science of New Thought

Watch our website for release dates

and order information!

www.wisewomanpress.com